Wisdom
of the
(S)Ages

BY DR. MICHAEL BERNARD

DORRANCE
PUBLISHING CO
EST. 1920
PITTSBURGH, PENNSYLVANIA 15238

Dorrance Publishing Co
585 Alpha Drive
Suite 103
Pittsburgh, PA 15238
Visit our website at *www.dorrancebookstore.com*

ISBN: 979-8-89127-884-4
eISBN: 979-8-89127-382-5

Wisdom

of the

(S)Ages

Contents

"Wisdom is the ability to see deeply into who people are and how they should move in the complex situations of life."

- David Brooks (*How to Know a Person*)

INTRODUCTION

You undoubtedly picked up this book because of the word "WISDOM"! Who wouldn't want to live with the wisdom to make ideal choices and move your life in a positive direction? You are also interested (as am I) in non-fiction books that you think will improve your understanding of life in general and hopefully promote your wellbeing in some practical ways. You may be a continual seeker of growth in the physical, emotional, mental, and spiritual areas of your life. On the other hand, you could be one of my friends or family members that will read this book because they feel obliged to.

My guess is that you do read fiction books when you want to relax and be entertained, but you always go back to a nonfiction book that will somehow promote your wellbeing and understanding and make life on this planet more fulfilling. You are probably always on the continual outlook for books, CDs, podcasts, TED talks, and teachings of the speakers and writers that you deem to be at the forefront in understanding what it takes to have a better, happier, more productive, and fruitful life.

For the first thirty-five years of my life, I couldn't have cared less about personal growth. In September of my 35th year, I was just trying to keep my head above water. I was in the sixth year of an alcoholic marriage and was told by a psychiatrist (one of many professionals that we were seeing) that I should divorce the "problem." I felt like I was in a deep pit with no way to get out. I couldn't even see the light at the top of the pit. The word "HOPE" was not in my mind or vocabulary. I had two small children who wanted and needed their mother, but she was not available and my reaction to her chemical use was one of resentment, disappointment, and frustration. This made my children's one available parent (me) angry, controlling, harsh, and unsuitable.

At the age of thirty-one, I finally had my first stable job. I had survived two years of professional school and was finally able to earn some money and pay off some debts. My two children did not come at a good time since my wife had physical problems as well as chemical problems. For most of the first four years out of my residency program, I was a single father with what seemed like THREE children while I tried to become known in the community and build my practice.

During the formative years of my life, I was never a spiritual person. Sure, I was taught that there was a "God," but my growth and daily problems were not something a Creator of the Universe would be concerned about. I enjoyed going to church but it was mostly because it was quiet and somehow gave me a comfortable feeling of belonging. I liked the music and it felt good to be in a place with so many other people who were not required to be there. My father was a Christian Scientist so as an only child, I went to his church. My mother also attended because that's what families are "supposed to do." In the forties and fifties, you went where your father told you to go and did what your father told you to do.

When I was a teenager, my father had gallbladder surgery. His church was opposed to their congregants going to physicians of any type and taking pre-scribed medications. So he either was "excommunicated" due to his medical procedure or just left the church, resenting being ostracized by the body of the church. He never returned to church after that and took up drinking to replace it. My mother was a Methodist before she met my father, so at the age of sixteen I was baptized for the first time in that church. At the age of seventeen, I left home to attend the college of my father's choice and never returned home except for a few months in the summer. I stayed away from home as much as possible or stayed alone downstairs in the recreation room and worked out with weights. I did this to avoid the repercussions from my father's drinking. He also was not very pleased that I was pursuing a pre-dental track in college rather than pre-law so I could follow in his footsteps.

Although my parents and relatives were well educated, they really had no desire to live a spiritually oriented existence. I saw no attempt to better themselves or others and they did not pass the concept of self-growth and improvement down to me. Most of what I observed was my father doing what made him feel good and my mother reacting to that. My childhood was really "good"—no violence, yelling, arguing, or animosity. But no real intimacy, compassion or love shown on a regular basis.

❖

When I realized I was sliding down into the pit of an alcoholic marriage, I really did not feel I had enough family support to seek refuge and solace there. I did mention to my mother in one instance that I thought my marriage was "in trouble." She gasped and indicated that it would "get better." I also brought it up to a good friend and he "didn't want to hear that stuff"!

As I was out of help and ideas, I went with the psychiatrist option of filing for divorce. The papers were served to my wife while she was in the hospital during one of her frequent admissions, and when she was informed that she would lose her two children in a divorce with her track record she decided to go to treatment.

While she was in treatment out of state, she called and said she would be attending AA but I would need to attend a program called Al-Anon. She didn't know what it was but like AA, it was a "spiritual" program and without it our relationship could not be rekindled and I would move on as a bitter, resentful, sarcastic divorcee.

Reluctantly, I faithfully attended an Al-Anon meeting each week. But it was more than six months before I realized that the weekly meetings and daily readings of Al-Anon literature was for me, not for my recovering wife. I began to understand that alcoholism was a disease and I also had a "disease"—one of COMPULSION and CONTROL. I had to fix the alcoholic and control the lives of other people in order to feel complete. I learned that the solution to my problems came through a spiritual outreach, embodied in the 12 Steps of both AA and Al-Anon. In the First Step, I was forced to admit that I was "powerless" over alcohol, my wife, my children, and others, and my life "had become unmanageable" in my futile attempts to assert my will.

The Second and Third steps gave me the answer to the question "Who was going to take care of my life and the people in my life if I could not do it?" Step Two asks us to "come to believe in a Power "Greater than ourselves."

Here, I had to dig up my distant relation to the God that I barely came to know as a youth and young adult through attending church. I learned to really pray for the first time in my life other than the rote words of formalized prayer. The Second Step promises a "return to sanity" if we can establish this belief in a "Higher Power." The Third Step asks us "to make a decision to turn our life and will over to this Higher Power" or "God as we understand Him." It is in this step that we learn to TRUST God and turn our lives and the lives of others over to him. The slogan for this in the program is "Let Go and Let God."

Those first three steps changed the course of my life. For the first time, I was not only growing spiritually but I was interested in personal growth in every phase. This included mental, emotional, and physical and well as spiritual change and growth. The Fourth Step is the first "action" Step, where you must make a "searching and fearless moral inventory" of yourself, with the idea of making changes for the better with God's help. In other words, a program of personal growth and positive change is the mainstay of the Al-Anon program and a life of "focusing on yourself" and serving others became the overriding purpose of my life.

The Serenity Prayer, prayed at each AA and Al-Anon meeting, asks God to "Grant me the serenity to ACCEPT the things I cannot change (mostly others and life as it happens), the courage to change the things I can (my attitude and life), and the WISDOM to know the difference." There is that word WISDOM, which is the subject of this book.

Now that I was a spiritual seeker, I had to totally revamp the life I was accustomed to living. I totally gave up the habit of looking at pornography when I was angry or upset with my lot in life. I joined the Catholic Church and faithfully followed its tenants, including weekly Mass and Reconciliation. I had been going to my wife's church since she was Catholic but never joined until I was in Al-Anon. I became a Godfather to my best friend's sixth newborn. I started teaching CCD or Sunday School at St. Paul's and was on the Confirmation Team.

I became more active in the local dental society and went through the chairs to become president. I helped my wife, who was now a very accomplished drug and alcohol counselor in the community, start a "Community Intervention" program in the local school system. I was the head of the "Dentists Concerned for Dentists" program at the Ohio Dental Association. I became a sponsor in Al-Anon and hosted our "Newcomers" meeting several times a year. All my activity was focused on advancing myself, my family, my profession, and my community, and to do this properly I needed help from those with more knowledge, foresight, and WISDOM than I possessed.

Of course, I sought the WISDOM of those around me, especially in the weekly Al-Anon and church meetings. But I had a desire to gain more understanding from those I couldn't meet with directly, and this is where I became a seeker of WISDOM through daily reading of books, listening to 8-track tapes and later CDs and videos.

In this book, I feature thirty "Sages" whose words of WISDOM have changed and enhanced my life. Most of them have many books and I have read many from some of the authors, but my goal is to feature the one book of theirs that has influenced and changed my outlook on life the most. I tried to list the authors and books in the order that I purchased and read or listened to them. When I peruse the list, it seems as if my reading started a little religious and business ordered and progressed to more spiritual and soul-enhancing themes.

This is probably because when I started my quest, I was just trying to learn how to function and live without resentment and frustration and I was trying to build my practice. As time went on, hopefully I would be able to stabilize my life and learn enough easy lessons that I could move on to a "higher" plane of living principles. The first books and tapes I can remember buying was in 1975, when I first joined the Al-Anon program. Now, almost forty-seven years later, I am still on my quest and buying books of the authors listed or listening to them on my Audible application as I drive nine hours a week to my two distant teaching jobs in Pennsylvania and Ohio!

I hope to relate how the book and author have influenced my life with the featured book and comments on some of the others he or she wrote. I hope to include some anecdotes of a personal nature to validate and emphasize the things I have learned. WISDOM is more than knowledge and understanding. It is the ability to make the right decisions and choices in life when circumstances are presented to us each day, one day at a time. My hope is that you will not only gain wisdom by reading this but believe that reading it was a wise decision.

OPTIMISM
THE POWER OF POSITIVE THINKING
NORMAN VINCENT PEALE

"Praying for people you do not like will do more for you than praying for those you love."

"Integrity, Courage, Enthusiasm, Happiness, Faith, Hope, Love: these are the key values to Live by."

Negativity was either my birthright or it was instilled in me from early childhood. Born at the start of World War II, when we had to ration sugar, gas, and other household items due to the war, I sensed that things were "not good" and would probably get worse. My parents seemed to exemplify the negative outlook that many people had in the early days of the war as well as starting their professional careers in the midst of the Great Depression of the thirties. The fact that I was their only child may be due to their reticence to bring any more children into this difficult time in our country's history.

Raised mostly by my mother, I can remember her best with her hand up to her cheek with a shocked or horrified expression on her face. This posture was often accompanied by a sigh or words of worry or concern. Since my parents have been gone for a long time, it is very easy to blame them for my negative outlook during the first half of my life, but like many others my philosophy was that if I planned for the worst, when it happened I wouldn't be upset. Except that I always was.

As I mentioned in the Introduction to this book, my "real" life began at age thirty-five, when the recovery program of Al-Anon jumpstarted me on a quest to improve the mental, emotional, and spiritual parts of my life. The first book I can remember reading was Norman Vincent Peale's *The Power of*

Positive Thinking. In fact, I may have even read it before my "real" life began because I always knew I tended to have a negative outlook on most everything, and I surmised that this short (218-page, soft-covered) book might help me with an "attitude adjustment."

Until I was married and my wife called me on my habit of "awfulizing," my negativity either didn't register or didn't bother me (or others) that much. If we were running late or if I was lost driving somewhere or was trying to fix something in the home beyond my job description, I would become extremely flustered, upset, and panicky. I used a four-letter word beginning with the letter "S" quite a bit. I may have received a mailing (since this was before email) from Norman Peale or his *Guideposts* ministry program informing me of his new book, *The Power of Positive Thinking*, and understanding that since I was really a "Negative Nelly" buying and reading this book might be of some help.

Maybe I liked the fact that Norman Peale was an Ohioan, as am I. I have always lived in the Northeast part of the state, and he was from the Southwest but he was still from "home." Of course, he moved to Pawling, New York, and most of his writing and ministering came from that part of the country. He was pastor of the Marble Collegiate Church on Fifth Avenue in New York City from 1932 to 1984. His initial book on *The Power of Positive Thinking* came out in 1952 and I estimate that I first read it about twenty years later, in the early 70s.

Through reading this book, I learned about "positive affirmations," both from the Bible and those I could make up myself. In the first chapter of his book, Norman quotes from the Bible using Paul's words to the Philippians (Chapter 4, Verse 13): "I can do all things through Christ who strengtheneth me." I have used that verse for fifty years, and it has helped me not only with positivity but knowing that I could succeed if I had faith in my convictions and my Higher Power. I now have positive affirmations that I looked up on Google, which I use as often as possible. Two of them that I use when I first arise are "I wake up happy and excited every single day!" and: "Each day of my life is filled with love and joy!" A few years ago, in my quest to be more positive, I taped a paper to my bathroom mirror with my four "Perfect, Purposeful 'P's." They are Perseverance, Patience, Posture, and POSITIVITY. I am deficient in all four of these qualities and have to remind myself to practice them each and every day.

The program of Al-Anon, as well as *The Power of Positive Thinking*, suggests that to create a more positive attitude one should make out a daily "Gratitude List." When we realize how many things are going well for us, it minimizes or puts into perspective the few things that are not going so well. Like many religious and self-improvement authors teach, one's thoughts are the key to one's attitude and behavior. As one of my Bible study participants liked to quote: "Thoughts are Things." A fearful thought can bring perspiration and a thought about dinner later tonight can produce increased salivation.

Because Norman Vincent Peale is a pastor, his teachings come from a Bible-based Christian point of view. Belief in the healing power of prayer and following Biblical principles is the most important way to a serene and worry-free life. From his book, I learned to "shoot" prayers at people. In other words, if you perceived someone was sad, upset, dour, or just having a rough time, focus on them and pray for them as if your prayer was being "shot" from your consciousness to theirs. You should also try this with difficult people or people you are at odds with. He even maintains that sometimes the person being "shot" by his prayer will turn around and look at him as if they feel the power and wonder where it came from. Norman Peale quotes in his book: "Personally I believe that prayer is sending out vibrations from one person to another and to God."

Two chapters in *The Power of Positive Thinking* that I like the best are chapters 7 and 8. Chapter 7 is "Expect the Best and Get It" and Chapter 8 is "I Don't Believe in Defeat." To go along with using positive thinking as a power, we are prompted to not just pray for things but to expect good things to happen and actually visualize ourselves as being successful in achieving the best outcome for us. According to Dr. Peale, we should always maintain an "Indomitable Spirit." Wikipedia states that "indomitable" means "incapable of being subdued, overcome, or vanquished." It means remaining upbeat even when things appear bleak, and if your goal is in accordance with God's will continue to pursue it at all costs no matter the obstacles. He is the only author that has used that concept, which leads to a positive and proactive approach to all situations.

The Power of Positive Thinking is divided into seventeen chapters, and all of the chapters end with seven or eight numbered suggestions at the end of the chapter to help one overcome or implement the chapter heading. As a consummate "people pleaser," one of my favorite chapters is "How to Get People to Like You." Some of the suggestions are: (1) Learn to remember names (one of my biggest defects!), (4) Be natural and normally humble, and (5) Practice liking people (people tend to like people who like them!).

Since my first reading of *The Power of Positive Thinking*, I have had subscriptions to *Guideposts* magazine from time to time and am still on the *Guideposts* mailing list as a member of the "Positive Thinkers Club" (monthly); the "Plus" pamphlets, which come in sets of three if you know how to properly separate them; and the "Prayer Power Club." This ministry allows you to list prayer requests, which are then prayed for by people in the *Guideposts* offices in Pawling, New York. Donations are at your discretion. Although both Norman and his wife are gone, Elizabeth Peale Allen, his daughter, is in charge of these publications.

Reading this book and practicing the religious principles outlined was my first step in my reach toward a "recovery" of the spiritual life and growth that would mark the next fifty years of my adult life.

DEDICATION
THE STRANGEST SECRET
EARL NIGHTINGALE

"Success is the progressive realization of a worthy ideal."

"The opposite of courage in our society is not cowardice—it is conformity."

When I began my self-improvement quest in the early seventies, I was just starting my career as an orthodontist. Since I was a partner in a business, I had to learn how to grow in that realm and not just as a religious or spiritual being. I really do not remember reading any of Earl Nightingale's books back then, but he was putting out albums of 8-track tapes on principles of leadership and business success that I listened to every time I traveled to and from work in my car.

For those younger than sixty, 8-track tapes came in "albums" of (usually) eight to twelve cassette tapes, which could be inserted into cassette recorders that cars finally featured back in the seventies. Once you had listened to the whole tape (thirty to forty-five minutes), you had to rewind it and then put in the following tapes to complete the entire program. There were no satellites back then so no Sirius radio or podcasts. There were no computer-downloaded programs like Amazon's Audible that you could use for long-drive listening. This was even before the era of CDs and even before the era of Blockbuster Video stores.

The first tapes I can remember listening to were either those of Earl Nightingale or ones produced by his recording company of other business and self-improvement lecturers. Earl had a low, rumbling voice, which was not only distinctive but somehow soothing and easy to listen to. My mother would have said he spoke like he had "tiny bubbles" coming out of his mouth. He was the first "mentor" that I listened to rather than just read articles and books they authored. Fifty years later, about 50 percent of my "self-improvement" learning is by listening to books and podcasts in my car through Audible or Sirius radio. As a parttime teacher at two schools, I drive between five and nine hours each week, which gives me much more time to soak up information from new authors at a much quicker pace than I was able to back in the Earl Nightingale tape days.

The book of Earl Nightingale's that I chose to refer to may not even be a real "book." It is comprised of a "Text of the Audio Version" of Earl's message and a smaller "Text of the Video Version." The message is actually an age-old belief that was formulated long before Earl Nightingale spoke about it. I know William James postulated it first in my references to the topic and much later it became extremely popular with a multitude of books and even movies featured on the premise. The modern version is just called *The Secret* (Rhonda Bryne) and few people today knew that it was Earl that made the concept practical and gave a list of ways to achieve success using it.

The "Secret" that has been written about for many decades is "We become what we think about." Although Earl's postulates are not totally from a religious viewpoint, he does quote Mark 9, Verse 23: "If thou canst believe, all things are possible to him (or her) that believeth." Many authors, some we will discuss later in this book, talk about the process of "visualization." This is picturing in your mind's eye what you want to happen and if you see it clearly and believe, it will come to pass. Jack Nicklaus, the famous golfer, would visualize his putt dropping in the middle of the hole before he took the stroke and felt a much-improved putting average. Many other athletes do the same thing, seeing themselves touching the finish line first in a running or swimming race. Many of the best athletes do this and it may be the difference between two competitors with the same talent. One believes and the other just competes. Earl states: "Picture yourself in your mind's eye as having already achieved the goal. See yourself doing the things you will be doing when you have reached your goal."

Of course, in order to achieve the desired goal you must first have a goal. The strangest secret in his text, really, is that only "one out of twenty" even has a goal. Your GOAL is what you think about positively when you want something to happen. How do you know if you have been successful if that success if not clearly defined? When I was in high school, I can't remember having clearcut goals. I went to college because my parents both had advanced degrees and enough money to send me. They also picked the college I would attend and were more excited than I was when I was accepted at the school of their choice.

Four years later, I went to dental school because I was told I was going to be a dentist by a school counselor whom I was sent to see because I was flunking out of pre-law. I joined the Air Force because all my dental school classmates were joining the service after dental school to ward off getting out into the world and making a living in a real business setting. The first actual personal goal I can remember was getting into an orthodontic program when my passion for that field was ignited by a mentor in my hospital residency.

When I first listened to Earl Nightingale's tapes as a young orthodontist, I immediately became goal-oriented. Each December I would set my goals for the year in five distinct categories: (1) Personal, (2) Family, (3) Practice, (4) Spiritual, and (5) Health. I would then list five or more mini-goals under each heading. For Personal, I might have "Read three fiction and three nonfictions books a month." For Family, "Pray nightly with my children and go to Wildwood on vacation in August." For Practice, "Meet monthly with my partner and attend two study clubs." For Spiritual, "Attend church weekly and two Al-Anon meetings weekly." For health, "Thirty minutes of cardio at the Y each morning and no food or drink after 8 P.M."

I have two confessions. The first is that I didn't review these goals on a regular basis; they were written in the back of my daily planner and in some years I only reviewed them in December, when I was inserting my new goals for the next year. The second is that I don't remember "visualizing" these goals. I have always had some trouble visualizing positive outcomes even though I have a pretty good imagination (refer to previous admission on negativity!). But I think just listing these objectives gave me the impetus to carry them out because I am a fairly regimented individual. Some would even say rigid or compulsive!

In his book and tapes, Earl Nightingale firmly believes one needs a "30-day program" to effectively promote a desired belief to come about. As mentioned, a formal written GOAL is the first necessity. The second thing is a good positive ATTITUDE (refer to Norman Vincent Peale). The third is the word THINK. Think deliberately with a purpose and write it down. Again, man (or woman) becomes what he or she thinks about most of the time. The next is to IMAGINE. Earl says, "to let your mind begin to soar." Then you need the COURAGE to CONCENTRATE on your goal every day. Here he sticks in the next concept of SAVING, because he is a firm believer in keeping a good financial balance and outlook. He would advocate saving 10 percent of what you earn.

The last principle he espouses is ACTION! This relates to the concept of SERVICE. It is impossible to be successful in any endeavor unless it serves someone or something. "Prosperity is founded upon a law of mutual exchange. Any person who contributes to prosperity must prosper in turn themselves. Sometimes the return will not come from those you serve, but it must come from someplace, because that is the law." I have always found the principle of serving others to be rewarding in that warm glow we get when we are uplifting those around us. It also stimulates others to "pay it forward" as Ohio State Coach Woody Hayes advocated to his players and students.

Even though I never thought of Earl Nightingale as a religious or spiritual mentor, his principle of "Believing Assures Achieving" is exemplified in his short 42-page book when he quotes from the Biblical "Sermon on the Mount" (Matthew 5, 6, 7).

> *"Ask, And it Shall be Given Unto You.*
> *Seek, And Ye Shall Find.*
> *Knock, And it Shall Be Opened Unto You,*
> *For Every One That Asketh Receiveth."*

Earl Nightingale was not only my first "audio" mentor, but his company produced audiotapes from many other self-improvement sages of the time. When he made reference to some of these pundits, I would either buy their book (or books) or would order the tape series so I could listen to them in my car. His writings and recordings may have been the impetus to keep me on the path of seeking a more productive and worthy way of life.

WINNING

THE PSYCHOLOGY OF WINNING
DR. DENNIS WAITLEY

"To win each day, make it your goal to play like The Superbowl! Focus all your energy on what and who you want to be."

"Everything in life is what you make it. It's not what is that counts, it's how you take it."

When I got to the grocery store this afternoon, I realized I had not made out a grocery list. Twenty-five years ago (or maybe even ten) I would have been upset, and fifty years ago I would have gone home and made one out. Today I smiled and shopped randomly, calmly picking up items I had no intention of buying and forgetting items I would have included on my small yellow legal-pad writing tablet.

Dennis Waitley would be appalled that I did not have a shopping list. Like most of the pundits I was influenced by forty or forty-five years ago, he is extremely organized, goal-oriented, and "all business." Dr. Waitley was greatly influenced by Earl Nightingale, and in his books on "Winning" (he has at least four with the word "winning" in the title) he credits Earl with the concept of "As you think and believe, so you will have or be." As Earl Nightingale was my first cassette tape mentor, I strongly believe that I first was influenced by Dennis Waitley from listening to his cassettes or teachings on programs through the Nightingale company.

Like the achievement-based business writers of that era, Dr. Waitley believed in focused planning, rigid determination, and strict regimens of upward striving. In life, he would identify three classifications of people. The vast majority are the SPECTATORS. They watch life happen as bystanders. They are not in the swim of things due to FEAR. They are afraid of failure but also of success because that carries the burden of responsibility and continued progress and effort. The second category is the LOSERS. Those people are the negative, self-critical, depreciating, unhappy followers of others. They tend to envy others and criticize others but are always putting themselves down as well. Obviously then, the WINNERS are the third category proposed by Dennis. These are the few (less than spectators or losers) who, in a very natural, free-flowing way, seem to get what they want. Again, the winners set GOALS and then use positive visualization and hard work to achieve those goals. Like his mentor, Earl Nightingale, the key difference between winners and losers is ATTITUDE. One's attitude toward one's potential is either the key to or the lock on the door of personal success and fulfillment.

In *The Psychology of Winning*, the author has ten small chapters on the traits required if you want to be labeled a "winner." All ten start with the words "POSITIVE" and "SELF." In other words, they are traits that are not only positive but are created for and by the individual for his or her personal growth and success. There are references to some of the people of his day whom he considers a winner. One of those is Orenthal James Simpson, otherwise known as O. J. Simpson. He brought himself up from an underprivileged kid to become a huge football star and commercial giant. Since the book was written in the 70s, it was twenty-five years before O. J. Simpson was charged with murdering his wife and later did jailtime for stealing! This might allude to the fact that winners can become losers if winning gives them too much power, money, and notoriety. Self-importance is not a positive trait.

In the first chapter on "Positive Self-awareness," Dr. Waitley states that winners are openminded. In the program of Al-Anon, those who grasp and benefit from the program are teachable. One of our slogans is "Listen and Learn." We also have guidelines against discussing politics, religion, or controversial issues while we are in the group meeting. We accept all people from all walks of life, and our primary (spiritual) aim is to aid people who desire to recover from the family disease of alcoholism and chemical dependency. The program teaches us compassion and empathy, which is also mentioned in the chapter on self-awareness.

At the end of each of the ten chapters, Dr. Waitley lists ten action steps to take each day to create the positive self-trait he discusses on the pages before.

I picked out the ones I thought would either be the most beneficial to any reader or the ones I had done myself or felt comfortable doing in the future. Some of the actions steps are: (1) Schedule a comprehensive annual physical exam, (2) Make a list of "I AM's" (affirmations), (3) Take thirty minutes each day for alone time, (4) Look for the truth and speak the truth, and (5) Be aware of the children and the elderly (me)!

The second of the ten chapters is on self-esteem. How one feels about oneself is the key to a worthy life. People who have the lowest self-esteem seem to be the ones who are offended the most easily. Also, the ones who yell loudest for service and attention are really calling for help because of low self-esteem. These last statements help us to understand more fully why some of the most important celebrities, politicians, and even former Presidents of the United States act out the way they do.

Winners don't need to defend themselves every time they are criticized. They focus on past successes, forget past failures, and use errors as a way to learn and move on. To be a winner, one needs to accept themselves as they are right now—an imperfect, changing, growing and worthwhile person. People with high self-esteem are accepting of themselves and others and have the ability to laugh at themselves and smile at and with others.

In the list of "to-dos" at the end of the chapter, Dr. Waitley promotes: (1) Be Grateful! Realizing your blessings puts your issues in true perspective, and (2) Stand tall with good posture. This is one of my failings even though I am short, and I have certain hallways at work where I remind myself to stand tall. Walking by windows and mirrors also helps. (3) Sit in the front row! This is the biggest lesson I can give my young and old students! I always sat in the front row because my name started with "B." I now do it partly because my eyesight and hearing are not what they used to be! But for people in a learning experience, sitting up front does two important things: (1) It shows the teacher that you are interested in them and the topic, and (2) It saves you from being distracted by those in front of you who are not involved in the learning experience.

This work on the principles of winning emphasizes the reliance on "yourself." Winners "make" it happen; losers "let" it happen. Winners want to do things to succeed, and losers have to do things to move forward. Most of the principles espoused by Dennis Waitley involve an inward drive of one's personal character. Chapters on self-control, self-motivation, self-discipline, and self-projection indicate a hard-charging reinvention of the personal psyche.

Hard-driving determination and relentless attention to elevating one's standing in the world is the key to the teachings of not only Dr. Waitley but many of the self-help speakers of his time.

Nowhere in the writing or teaching is there any mention of religion or spirituality. Earl Nightingale referred to the Bible and other mentors and groups, but Waitley's teachings in this volume are more "self-oriented," as all ten chapters indicate. When I was influenced by Dr. Waitley's cassette tapes back in the day, I was more concerned about elevating myself, especially in my business, by myself, and "winning" as a business owner and dental specialist was most important. His philosophy of "Winning isn't the most important thing, it's the only thing!" and "You play to win the game!" are almost foreign concepts to me today.

Through the Al-Anon program, I have become a bit more relaxed and accepting. One of our daily readers talks about recovering from "grim determination" and giving up control. I have learned the process of "surrender," which was almost an unheard-of concept when I was a young professional in a competitive profession. I am more inclined to ask for help from others and as a result of the program, I have a sponsor who mentors me and sets me straight when he thinks my "self-importance" is showing up. I try to meditate now using the *Calm* app on my phone and pray a lot to my Higher Power, whom I call God. My prayer always reflects the Eleventh Step when I "pray for his will for me and the power to carry it out."

My more self-accepting, self-relaxing, letting-go posture may come partly from being retired and no longer in the "competitive" arena of business. But I still have goals and objectives as a teacher, writer, and mentor. I'm just not as hardcore driven to "achieve." Would Dr. Waitley classify me as a winner today? Probably not, but I am happier and more content no matter how I am classified.

ACHIEVING
OVER THE TOP
ZIG ZIGLAR

"The solution to a problem I had wrestled with for three solid months came to me when I completely forgot about my needs and became engrossed in finding a way to meet the need of others."

"It was character that got us out of bed, commitment that moved us into action, and discipline that enabled us to follow through."

Zig Ziglar's first well-known book was *See You at the Top*. The obvious follow-up was this book, *Over the Top*. I never read either book until just finishing *Over the Top* this week. Zig is a businessman with a background in selling and his philosophy is geared toward that industry, although his teachings are practical for any career or endeavor.

As mentioned before, the only book I had read up to this point in my "self-improvement" outreach was by Norman Vincent Peale. The other authors referred to were listened to on 8-track cassette tapes. Most of those were purchased through the Earl Nightingale-Vic Conant series of motivational and self-promotion programs. Zig Ziglar was not someone I had heard of through my profession or from my own research, but when I heard his message on tapes from the Nightingale-Conant series I resonated with his philosophy. I only listened to these cassette tapes in my car, so I am fortunate that I drive a lot. Currently, I drive nine hours on two weeks of each months and five hours on the other three. If I had driven that much back in the seventies, when I listened to Zig's words, I would be much farther ahead today.

In *Over the Top*, Zig Ziglar references some of the previous authors who were instrumental in starting me on my self-improvement quest. He was influenced by both Dennis Waitley and Norman Vincent Peale although, like Dr. Peale, he is a strong believer in "God," having made a strong commitment in 1972. Of course, I relate to this "coming to God" moment myself since it happened to me in 1975, when my wife entered the AA program and I began learning how to live in the Al-Anon program. The first three steps in the program instruct you to

"come to believe" in God and then "turn your life and will over to that Higher Power or God." At this point in my life, I knew that whatever improvement I was able to make in my life had to be in accordance with the wishes of the "God of my understanding."

Being a businessman, Zig also referenced another salesman named Walter Hailey, an insurance agent with likeminded skills in promoting, motivating, and selling. As a dentist, I never thought I would need any business models or courses in sales but soon found out that dentistry was a business that needed these skills as well as any other business. An orthodontist in Texas, where Walter Hailey lived, decided that Walter, founder of Planned Marketing, should be a teacher and mentor to orthodontists and dentists. Thus, a program called "Dental Boot Kamp" was started in the late 70s. Since I was then on my quest to elevate my orthodontic practice as well as my own self-esteem and self-awareness, I signed up for a week with Walter and eight or ten other orthodontists in the Hill Country of Texas.

We had to write positive affirmations about the other participants even though we didn't really know them and then look at these reinforcing kudos every morning of the course. We also had to walk in the dark at 6 in the morning with a walking "buddy" (another orthodontist). We were to walk for a half-mile with one of us talking about ourselves and our dreams and then on the half-mile back, the other professional would do all the talking. Coupled with Peale's Positive Thinking, this practice of Positive Acting really kickstarted me on my way to be more positive about my practice and personal life.

Like the other mentors I have already referenced, Zig was most concerned about setting GOALS! His phrase or acronym for this concept was "Godly Objectives Assure Lasting Success." Since being in the Al-Anon program, where relationship to God or a Higher Power is always necessary, I am always comforted when motivational sages refer to God and reinforce the need to rely on God.

Many motivational speakers like Zig Ziglar influence people with PASSION and ENTHUSIASM. A book I read years ago on the qualities of a good teacher indicated that enthusiasm was the best attribute for a teacher to have in order to influence his or her students. Although I never saw Zig perform, he confesses that he jumps up and down and is very animated when he gives talks on his philosophy of life and growth.

Zig Ziglar's book emphasizes the importance of positive self-talk and even has pages of positive statements for the reader to read daily or memorize to be used at any time. One of my favorite books he discusses in this vein is *The Little Engine that Could*. Saying the words "I think I can" is great but even better is repeating the phrase "I know I can" over and over to yourself.

Creating a personal "Mission Statement" and "Vision" is incredibly important, along with having the COMMITMENT and DISCIPLINE to adhere to them. Zig talks about such commitment that when he was a runner, he ran every morning at 6 A.M. and one night he didn't get home until 4 A.M. but still ran two hours later because of both discipline and commitment. At the time that I first heard Zig's tapes, I was not only younger but more rigid and compulsive. I certainly would have followed his example but now, the Al-Anon program has taught me the concept of "Easy does it" and "How important is it?" I am self-assured enough now to miss a running day to rest and relax and not feel like my whole exercise program is for naught. On this same vein, he mentions an eighth-grader who flunked and was made to repeat the grade. Although he was angry and embarrassed, he went on to become a very successful CEO of a major company. One of my four children had poor grades in the eighth grade as well, but instead of making him repeat and face bullying from the students we found him a private school that could tend to his educational needs. Discipline has to have a soft side to it, in my opinion.

This book was written when Zig Ziglar was in his 70s, so he referenced the goals of senior citizens like me. The four fundamentals as a retiree or senior are GRATITUDE for a long life, continual LEARNING regardless of your age, daily EXERCISE to maintain physical and mental health, and HELPING OTHERS. Thanks to the Al-Anon program, the North Canton YMCA, researching the authors for this book, and my volunteer work at the Church of the Lakes and Akron Children's Hospital, I check all four boxes.

SUCCESSFUL
MY PHILOSOPHY FOR SUCCESSFUL LIVING
JIM ROHN

"Taking time to sit down and write out your goals for the present, the near future and the more remote future is a necessary part of transforming your life."

"Find a way to serve many people! Simply stated, this is what leads to great wealth, great power, and great influence."

In the mid-seventies, I was regularly buying cassette tape programs from the Nightingale Company and was deeply into "self-development," as Jim Rohn calls it. Again, I never read a book by Jim Rohn until I purchased and read *My Philosophy for Successful Living* so I could revisit the things I learned from this businessman-turned-success-builder.

Like Earl Nightingale, Jim Rohn had a distinctive voice that made listening to him more pleasing and entertaining. Unlike Earl's slow, deep delivery, Jim had a more businesslike, rapid staccato that seemed to indicate confidence, knowledge, and wisdom. His little book on successful living was very short and one could read it in an hour, but there is a lot of content in these few pages.

After reading the books by these five initial sages that jumpstarted my concern about self-development or self-improvement in the 70s and 80s, I realized that there are two principles that are shared and emphasized by all five. They are (1) Set GOALS, and (2) SERVE OTHERS! Goals should be written and given timeframes. Current goals should be written and kept on your phone or tablet to review constantly. Future goals (five-year, ten-year) should be written and kept in your computer or journal and reviewed every six months or at least once a year. As Jim Rohn states: "Find a way to serve many people! Simply stated, this is what leads to great wealth, great power, and great influence." He also references Zig Ziglar's principle of "forgetting about your needs and become completely engrossed in serving the needs of others." If someone endorses and encompasses these two principles in their lives, they will have uncommon success and advanced personal growth and satisfaction.

Many of these "initial sages" in my early development years did not talk about a Higher Power of "God of their understanding." In my own development I was a neophyte in a daily program of prayer and faith in God, so this matched my level of understanding at the time. Jim Rohn even admits he is "an amateur on the topic" but this comes in the last few pages of his little book and is not even listed under the category as "spiritual development," which he says is crucial. But he does discuss "planting the seed and allowing God to do the rest." In the back of the book, there is a written text of an interview that Jim had with another self-development sage. Both men were asked what book they read that elevated their understanding of life and success the most. The one being interviewed with Jim said, *"Think and Grow Rich."* Surprisingly, when the interviewer turned to Jim Rohn, he stated that it was the Bible that helped him the most.

Back in the days that I read these books, I was building my orthodontic practice and I was somewhat concerned about monetary success. This book by Jim Rohn fits into that mode very well in that he started his "self-education" at twenty-five and by the time he was thirty-one he was a millionaire. He maintains that he understood the fact that "a formal education gets you a job, but 'self-education' is what make you rich." His philosophy is that if you work hard on your job you can make a good living, but if you work hard on yourself you can make a fortune. His goals in this self-development are great wealth, great power, and great influence.

Money and wealth accumulation was never a motivator for me, even in the lean years when I first began my practice and my drive to better my mental, emotional, physical, and spiritual self. In my practice I did try to improve my profits and keep track of how much money the practice made, but that was more of an indicator of practice success than it was a "wealth accumulation" process. I also wanted to be able to uplift my employees with above-average compensation and practice perks, so making enough to hire and treat people well was a motivating factor.

Speaking of uplifting employees, Jim Rohn felt they were the key to your success and the three things you needed to do for them included (1) Training, (2) Teaching, and (3) Inspiring. Teaching was my strong point, and it was my office employees' validation of my teaching efforts that led me to take two jobs in retirement teaching young orthodontic residents what I had learned in forty-six years of practice. As we say in the Al-Anon program, I try not to give them too much advice but use my "experience, strength, and hope" to ensure a better orthodontic career and a more successful life.

Since Jim Rohn did mention the importance of the Bible, that will be the next book I will make reference to and the beginning of books I have read thoroughly rather than just listen to on cassette tapes, CDs, or digital programs.

TEACHABILITY
THE SERMON ON THE MOUNT
THE GOSPEL OF MATTHEW –
NEW TESTAMENT IN THE BIBLE

"When someone strikes you on (your) right cheek, turn the other one to him as well."

"If you forgive others their transgressions, your heavenly Father will forgive you. But if you do not forgive others, neither will your Father forgive your transgressions."

Admittedly, the Bible wasn't one of the first books I picked up on my quest to focus on personal development at age thirty-five, when my wife started in AA and I accepted that Al-Anon was a way of life from which I could benefit. I knew a few Bible stories, but I don't think I even had a Bible in the house at that time. I prayed very little and my spiritual life was nonexistent, although I was made aware that Al-Anon was a "spiritual program."

One of the first things I did in 1975 was to commit myself to the church that I was attending since my son just went through his First Communion. After I was confirmed in the Catholic Church, I thought one of the ways I could serve the church and get closer to God was to teach Sunday School or CCD, as it was called in the church at that time.

Since I was not a "Cradle Catholic" I had little knowledge of the rites and rituals of Catholicism, but I was told by my office staff that I was a good teacher so I decided to volunteer to educate the eighth-grade class, the same age of the patients that I had been treating for four years in my orthodontic practice. Since I made that commitment, I thought it would be a good idea to buy a Bible and read it so I could impart its wisdom to my eighteen or twenty Sunday morning students. The Bible I used at that time was the "Catholic Bible," and I even read the whole text in a year as a part of a formalized plan. Now that I am no longer a Catholic I use "The Message," which is the Bible in contemporary language, which was put together by Eugene Peterson.

Once I became familiar with the Old and New testaments, I would tell my students each year that they really did not have to read the entire Bible to gain wisdom and a spiritual understanding. Most of the guidelines of spiritual and altruistic living can be found in just two books. In the Old Testament, reading the book of Proverbs that was written by Solomon would give them short bullet points on proper attributes and behavior, and in the New Testament the book of Matthew, especially chapters 5, 6, and 7, were most important. These verses, known as the Sermon on the Mount, was where Jesus lectured his disciples and onlookers on God's plan for loving and living the right way.

The first "hero" in the Old Testament was Joseph, son of Jacob. In the first book of Genesis he is sold into slavery by his own brothers, then put in jail after resisting temptation from his slaveowner's wife. He puts up with brotherly bullying and tormenting, does the right thing after being accused of sexual advances and still gets punished. Throughout these ordeals, he remains faithful in his belief and prayers to God, and eventually good things begin to happen and he is elevated to first-in-command in Egypt under the Pharaoh. The biggest lesson in his story is one of FORGIVENESS because when the brothers come back to Egypt to ask for food during a famine, he is able to overlook what they did to him twenty years ago and give them the food they need. The lesson: Good things happen when we accept what is and remain faithful and prayerful in both the hard times as well as the good times.

Many would cite David as an Old Testament hero because he was chosen by God to be king, and as a youth he killed the Philistine giant Goliath. But I would teach my class that the true hero was David's best friend and son of King Saul, Jonathon, who demonstrated LOYALTY to David when he protected him from his father, King Saul, who was trying to eliminate the popular David. He saved David's life against his own father's wishes, knowing that if David lived David would become king rather than the rightful heir, Jonathon.

Of course, COMMITMENT to God was shown in the stories of Shadrack, Meshack, and Abednego, who were thrown in a fiery furnace, and Daniel, who was placed overnight in a lion's den because they refused to bow down to earthly kings in favor of the God of the universe. These four men were unharmed, offering proof of who God was and what he could bring about for those that worshipped Him.

In the New Testament, the teachings of the Messiah, Jesus, are featured, starting with the gospel of the author, Matthew. All four writers of the four gospels relate similar stories of Jesus' life and teachings in his three years of ministry with slight variations. In Matthew, Jesus first addresses his disciples and followers on "The Mount," whereas in the gospel of Luke his first sermon is on "The Plain."

Matthew's account of Jesus' first address starts with the "Beatitudes," or actions that bring about blessings from God. According to the Bible (the Message), "You're blessed when you are content with who you are." As a recovering perfectionist, I have always had trouble being "content" with who I am and how things are progressing in my life! "You're blessed when you show people how to cooperate instead of compete." Again, my competitive nature often searches the orthodontic community to see what my standing is. One of the Beatitudes where I might pass is "Keep open house; be generous with your lives. By opening up to others, you'll prompt others to open up with God." I surmise myself to be generous, at least financially, in all instances and reaching out to others in most circumstances.

After the "blessing" part of the Sermon, according to Matthew, Jesus tells his followers (and us) to "watch what we say because words can kill." I would teach my eighth-graders that the Old Testament Commandment "Thou shall not kill" could be broken simply by using hurtful words to friends or family members. Jesus warns us to "do something for someone else rather than call attention to yourself."

His teachings further instruct us "not to say anything you don't mean" and to "just say yes when you mean yes and no when you mean no." Some of the hard teachings regard taking a blow to the cheek and, rather than retaliating, turn your other cheek. No tit for tat! His instruction to love your enemies is not an easy platitude either. I really can't think of many personal enemies for me to love, but there are a whole lot of political characters that I have trouble loving and even accepting.

Matthew tells us that Jesus is extremely focused on forgiving everyone and indicates that if we do not forgive His (and our) Father in Heaven will not forgive us. We are to "not be so preoccupied on getting so we can respond to

God's giving." And of course, Matthew emphasizes Jesus' use of the golden rule. "Ask yourself what you want people to do for you, then grab the initiative and do it for them." Some other teachings that Matthew records are "Don't pick on people or criticize their faults." Most sages believe there is no such thing as constructive criticism. One of the hardest things to do is to point out to a friend or associate where they may be getting off course without seeming critical or condescending. Jesus tells us to "Ask for what we need. Be direct and don't bargain with God."

Besides the Gospel of Matthew, many of the letters written by Paul in the New Testament give us spiritual direction for a fulfilling life. My favorite is the letter to the Philippians, although the "love chapter" in Corinthians is not only true and classic but is recited at more than half of wedding ceremonies.

Using the Bible daily as I do now creates a closer bond to the God of my understanding, improves my spirituality and faith and gives me Good Orderly Direction (GOD) in how to satisfactorily relate to others and live my life in peace and harmony. On Sundays I attend a Bible-based Methodist Church and on Mondays I am blessed to be in two Bible studies. In the mornings, I have three male friends who have met for over thirty years in a group started among "Young Life" committee members. In the afternoons, I am in a mixed group of about twelve members of our Methodist Church. My spiritual growth over the past forty-seven years is directly related to Al-Anon, prayer, Bible study, and the wisdom of the sages.

WISDOM
CHANGE YOUR THOUGHTS, CHANGE YOUR LIFE DR. WAYNE DYER

"You get what you think about, whether you want it or not!"

"What other people think about me is none of my business."

Of all the many sages I have read or listened to over the last forty-seven years, Wayne Dyer is the one I related to the most. He is also the only sage I will cover that I was so influenced by that I read many of his books, listened to practically all his tapes and CDs and even watched at least one of his videos.

My connection with him is somewhat personal, not just philosophical. We were very close in age, with Wayne being born in 1940 and me living for two and a half months in 1939. In our early adult years we were both driven and compulsive, although some of Wayne's earlier writings (*Your Erroneous Zones*) seemed a bit out of touch with the spirituality I was trying to develop. Like me, Wayne was a committed runner and even tended to "brag" that he ran for an eight-year stretch without missing a day! Like Wayne, I would run on days that I was tired or hurt because I didn't want to admit any weakness and break a streak that meant so much to me at the time. I was goal-oriented and a "striver" and I perceived that he was as well. Commitment was overly important to both of us.

During Dr. Dyers' early years as a teacher and writer, he was dealing with the disease of addiction to alcohol. I tried to be an alcoholic but failed and finally quit completely when my wife went to treatment for her addiction and I decided to give up alcohol as a part of my quest to become healthier mentally, physically, emotionally, and spiritually. Wayne also was able to overcome his disease, although I am not sure if he was in a program of recovery or not. My wife was in AA for many years before her relapse and I am still in Al-Anon today, which has been the biggest influence in my spiritual growth and development.

Many of the tapes and CDs I listened to from Dr. Dyer also featured other sages that I related to. He had some great ones with Marianne Williamson, Deepak Chopra, and Eckhart Tolle, among others. Since he wrote so many books, I choose one for this writing that I really never read. I did listen to his CDs on this topic and became enamored with his interpretation of the Tao Te Ching in his book: *Change Your Thoughts, Change Your Life – Living the Wisdom of the Tao*. This offering is an example of how Dr. Wayne Dyer "softened" and become more Spirit-oriented as he traveled along in his career as a sage. Since the same thing was happening to me, I continued to relate to his lectures and philosophy. Dr. Dyer passed away at the tender age of seventy-five of cancer, but his thoughts and wisdom will live on forever.

Dr. Dyer's interpretation of Lao-tzu's 81 lessons from 2,500 years ago resonated strongly with me both now and at the time I listened to it. As I mentioned, my spirituality was on the upswing not only due to Al-Anon and the Twelve Steps, but also the books and programs I was selecting were more spiritual in nature. The initial sages I listened to were more about business and achievement and were goal-oriented and involved dynamic action. Now we come to the "Tao" and goals are not that important. Rather than being loud and aggressive, we are taught by Lao-tzu and Dr. Dyer to be soft, flexible, and in the background.

> *The great leader speaks little,*
> *He never speaks carelessly.*
> *He works without self-interest*
> *and leaves no trace.*
> *When all is finished, the people say,*
> *"We did it ourselves."*

This 17th verse of the 81 in the "Tao" is an example of the philosophy of "less is more." He prompts us to speak little and stay in the background with humility. Dr. Dyer referred to Spirit or God often and surmises that Lao-tzu meant the Tao to be our Higher Power, God, or "the Mother of all things."

The author and the Al-Anon program agree that we are to "Let go and let God" (Tao).

Unlike some of the other sages like Andy Andrews, who indicated that we are to "Do Something," the Tao urges us to "Do Nothing." Obviously, if I am having a heart attack in front of you I would hope you would "Do Something." On the other hand, the Tao states that we should "Do Nothing" and simply ALLOW! Surrender is better than constantly trying to create the optimum outcome.

In my daily reading of topics from the "Daily Word" from Unity, the term Divine Order is used to indicate that all things are in God's hands, and we are to allow this natural order to play out without resistance or concern. The Tao even warns us to "Stop chasing your dreams" (or goals) and "be accepting." Flow versus struggle. One of my Al-Anon friends recites the child's verse "Row, row, row your boat, gently down the stream" as to how we are to react to life's travails. The Tao would not only have us flow gently but we would not even need to row.

> Trying to control leads to ruin.
> Trying to grasp, we lose.

This 29th of the 81 verses of the Tao warns us to give up control. Lao-tzu uses water a lot in his verses and trying to grasp water is a futile effort as is anything else in our lives. The Al-Anon program is for people who are addicted to "control." We have tried to control the alcoholic, our children, our employees, our neighbors, and we have to develop a trust in a Higher Power so we can relinquish that control to Him or Her and thus achieve serenity and a quiet mind and heart.

Wayne Dyer's quote from one of his programs before this one on the need for approval is "What other people think about me is none of my business." Approval addiction has been one of my shortcomings and I still have trouble getting over it. According to the Tao, the "chase" for adoration, money, and power is a waste because there will never be enough to satisfy the person in need. He says that those who need approval the least seem to receive it the most.

Although Lao Tzu has a softer, gently approach to life with emphasis on compassion and no violence, he agrees (according to Dr. Dyer) that uplifting others is the pathway to success and fulfillment. We are to "See God in everyone we encounter."

One with true virtue
Always seeks a way to give.
One who lacks true virtue
Always seeks a way to get
To the giver comes the fullness of life;
to the taker, just an empty hand.

This 79th of the 81 verses of the Tao agrees with all of the other sages that success comes from giving or making sure others achieve success. Uplifting our fellow man has been an instruction for a rewarding life for the past 2,500 years and will continue to be for the next 2,500. Living "low" like Jesus Christ, Buddha, Mohammad, Gandhi, Nelson Mandela and other leaders and teachers is the philosophy of the Tao as interpreted by Dr. Wayne Dyer.

Beside the universal teaching of all sages to "lift up other people," the title of Dr. Dyer's book is a philosophy that the Tao and the other sages agree upon. As Wayne says in this book and others: "I get what I think about whether I want it or not."

ATTRACTING
THE KEY TO LIVING THE LAW
OF ATTRACTION JACK CANFIELD

"Simply put, the Law of Attraction says that you will attract into your life whatever you focus on."

"Beliefs are just your habitual thoughts, and they can be changed through affirmations, positive self-talk, behavioral changes, and visualization techniques."

The reason I purchased Jack Canfield's book on the *Law of Attraction* was because it was small, thin, and contained only 135 pages. It was probably purchased and read around the same time as Wayne Dyer's work on changing your life by changing your thoughts because basically, that is the Law of Attraction. It follows James Allen's philosophy that "a man is as he thinketh." The books and movies on the "Secret" were just coming out, and of course we learn that the Secret is basically "what you think about expands." You create your own destiny by the power of your thoughts. If you fill your mind with negative thoughts, your days and nights will not be very good. On the other hand, if you rule out negativity and ponder on good things and envision positive outcomes, your life can be one of fulfillment and joy.

We immediately see some similarities in the wisdom found in this book and some of our past authors. Jack Canfield states early on that faith in a "Higher Power" is paramount to the practice of this process of thought processing. In the introduction, he maintains that the Law of Attraction is the scientific explanation for coincidence, serendipity, and the power of prayer. Almost all the sages to this point have a spiritual bend or have developed one, which is exemplified in their writing.

The other common thread among the first seven authors is the idea of setting GOALS. Wayne Dyer definitely believes in setting goals but in referencing the Tao Te Ching, it would appear that most of its philosophy leads one to just flow and allow instead of setting goals, which would cause you to "strive" for an outcome that you desired. To counter that concept, Jack Canfield emphasizes that to let life just "happen" to you is irresponsible.

All energy follows thought. It is always our choice as to what that thought should be. Not thinking is virtually impossible. Since we have our choice of positive or negative thought, we are taught in Canfield's book that we should choose optimism, gratitude, and joy to enhance our lives. Negative thoughts bring negative emotions such as hatred, anger, jealousy, and fear.

Negativity has always been my default mode. I'm really not sure if that was inherited or developed over time but it appears that this may be true for all people. To have a positive outlook on everything is something that must be developed and worked on, whereas being negative or complaining, comparing, and criticizing are habits that are extremely easy and comfortable falling back into.

One of my habits that leads to negative thinking is watching the daily news on TV and reading (sometimes two) papers to see what is going on. Obviously, most of the news is bad because it attracts more readers and listeners, so when I am done reading two papers and watching the evening local and national news I am angry, fearful, disgusted, and downhearted, and this definitely creates a hit in my self-esteem and confidence in humanity. One good thing about the nightly NBC national news is that they end the half-hour segment with an "Inspiring Moment," which is the only positive feature that portrays a heartwarming, encouraging event. I never turn the TV off until I have seen that last segment because I come away feeling better about mankind and myself after that.

The other habit I have fallen into lately is watching "true crime" shows on TV. In these one-hour dramas, someone gets killed (always) and the first half-hour is devoted to finding out who did it. The second half-hour is the trial of the charged suspect, which is the part I enjoy the most. However, it is very negative, not just the killing but the anger and vitriol of the people involved along with the portrayal of fear and retribution. Giving up the newspaper since I am retired would be very difficult, but giving up these negative-thought-producing TV dramas would be easy and is one of my current goals. Reading the comics in the newspaper does bring some uplifting or at least humorous thoughts after acknowledging all the bad news.

I am told that the social media sites all have algorithms that lean toward the negative side because that is what the consumer enjoys reading and hearing about. In my attempt to escape a negative mindset I do not use any of the social media sites, nor do I go to violent movies or play videogames where the object is to kill or be killed.

As I write this, I am in a divorce support group in my church since I experienced a divorce five years ago. Our goal is to take a negative experience that has occurred or is occurring in the lives of the participants and teach them to respond and not react. They learn that forgiveness is necessary for them to release pent-up anger and thus create a path to recovery and a better life. They are so wounded by their faulty thinking that they will never be able to create a fulfilling life for themselves until they go through this thought-changing process. We ask them to make no major decisions or get into any romantic relationships for a year because reversing the thought process takes time.

The last half of Jack Campbell's book is a blueprint for developing the goals that you need to create the life you want. Finding your purpose is important, so you need to fill out an information sheet (provided) on the gifts you possess, your known skills, and what you love to do. Since thoughts will get you what you desire, you need to dream big.

Once you list your goals, you must constantly think on how you will achieve each one. The goal must be positive rather than negative or the Law of Attraction will not work. In other words, the goal must be "I see myself as a nonsmoker" rather than "I will not smoke another cigarette." When I was practicing, I always had goal categories such as (1) personal, (2) physical, (3) practice, (4) family, and (5) spiritual, but after setting them on January first I never really thought about them until I happened on them months later in my journal. The Law of Attraction says that if I really want them, I need to think positively about them every day.

Along with goals, Affirmations, Visualization, and Attitude are important on a daily basis if you are to create the best life. Get up in the morning and look in the mirror and tell yourself (out loud) that you will have a great, successful day. I found some affirmations by Googling "affirmations" online, and Jack Canfield has a list in the book. Some of his are (1) "My life is filled with love and beauty," (2) "I am divinely guided and protected," and (3) "I am attracting joy into my life." Mel Robbins, a sage that I will review later, wrote a book called *The High 5 Habit*, which is the best book on positive daily affirmations to jumpstart a great day.

Visualization has always been hard for me. The first time I ever heard of the concept was when I found out that Jack Nicklaus always envisioned his putt going into the center of the cup before he actually took the shot! Since the premise is that thoughts are more important than actions, you can actually think of a positive outcome in advance and it will manifest more often than not. One of the participants in a Bible study that I am in maintains that "thoughts are things." To exemplify this, he tells the group that he now has an (imaginary) lemon in his hands and is cutting down through the juicy fruit and the sour liquid is dripping out. "Is there anyone in the group that did not have an increase of saliva in their mouth just thinking about that process?"

An "Attitude of Gratitude" is the most positive way to achieve success. Trusting God to provide and believing that He wants you to have the fruition of your wants and dreams is paramount in your successful pursuit of the Law of Attraction. Jack Campbell even sells "Vision Books" and "Gratitude Journals," which enable the reader to use the techniques of goal setting, visualization, and gratitude in practicing these principles every day.

ENHANCING
THREE THINGS SUCCESSFUL PEOPLE DO
JOHN C. MAXWELL

"If you make happiness your goal, you are almost certainly destined to fail."

"Success is knowing your purpose in life, growing to reach your maximum potential, and sowing seeds that benefit others."

The second quote on page nine in John C. Maxwell's book is really the entire essence of his 200-page message. His main premise is that we are all born to do something specific that will enhance our life and the lives of others. Our objective is to find out what that purpose is and then work tirelessly toward optimizing it continuously.

Like many of the other authors or sages that will be outlined in this book, John is a pastor who uses his belief in God and his preaching pulpit to encourage the reader and follower to be the best we can be, especially in a leadership role. Many of his books are on leadership because he strongly believes that you cannot just benefit yourself through personal growth but have an obligation to uplift as many others as possible as well. He wants others "to come along for the ride" that you provide with continued growth and leadership skills.

We are now into our ninth sage and eight of them talk extensively about the habit of setting GOALS. The only sage that wrote a book that was not goal-oriented was Wayne Dyer, whose reference to Lao Tzu in the Tao Te Ching was more about "allowing" than "creating." However, many of Dr. Dyer's books discuss the idea of goals and "manifesting" or creating the life you desire rather than leaving success be a product of random chance or serendipity.

The title of John Maxwell's book references three things you need to do to be successful. The simplified version of those three are: (1) Know your purpose, (2) Focus on growing to your maximum potential, and (3) Sow seeds that benefit others. In other words, we all have a specific journey in life for which we are best equipped. We need to find out what this is and then work diligently to maximize that gift or outreach. Once we are successful with that endeavor, we use it to benefit and uplift others. We use our leadership skills to bring others along with us so they can have the growth and success that we have created for ourselves.

My life is a little like that right now. I retired from my active orthodontic practice in December of 2016. I really didn't want to retire because I loved what I did and loved the patients I was able to influence in appearance, function, and future. Since we were bringing in a new orthodontist whom we wanted in our practice, my current partner made me set a retirement date so our two-doctor practice would not struggle with three doctors for an undetermined time.

Because I wanted to retire to something rather than from something, I decided to use my forty-six years of experience to teach at two orthodontic residencies, in Ohio and Pennsylvania. When I became a parttime clinical professor, I realized that as much as I loved practicing orthodontics I really enjoyed teaching it to the young millennial residents at both schools. I truly believe that teaching is my talent and purpose, and even at my advanced age in life and in the profession I am trying to maximize my knowledge and expertise in order to create the best possible learning environment for the young doctors under my charge.

Since teaching is my talent and purpose and I realized both of these things later in life, there is ample proof that it is never too late to find one's true calling in life and then maximize it to the fullest extent in order to lead and lift others. My only regret now is that I did not teach while I was still in practice so I would be able to physically do the things I am teaching along with the new concepts in my orthodontic profession.

As mentioned before, I taught Sunday School for thirty-five years, taught two sets of children in two different generations at home and taught my dental assistants and practice team how to run an orthodontic practice. The chairside assistants always told me I was a good teacher. I should have paid more attention to them and focused more on honing my skills and using them to fulfill my purpose.

Another similarity that John C. Maxwell has with previous reported sages is the idea that "thinking can make it so." He quotes Henry Ford with that premise and he feels that a good, positive attitude, along with persistence, will lead the individual to success. So, what is success? According to Maxwell, success is helping others as well as continuous "self-development."

Self-development is the most important character of a leader. Maxwell is "always working" to become better and seems to never rest in that pursuit. He tells the story of flying on an airplane and while he is busily writing, studying, and learning, the passenger in the seat next to him is either snoozing or reading the airline magazine. He doesn't take them to task out loud for "chilling" when they could be working "on themselves" but indicates that the winners are constantly working and the losers are taking time off.

Obviously, his life is one of intense discipline! He uses the "one hour a day" plan. On Monday he spends one hour with a devotional, Tuesday one hour listening to a leadership recording, Wednesday is one hour filing quotes and reflecting on the leadership lesson. The rest of the week may find him writing, reading the Bible or other books of knowledge.

John Maxwell's goals are referred to as "mile markers" to show him that he is on the road to leadership success. These goals need to be written, measurable, achievable, and time sensitive. When we do not achieve our goals, the prime reason may be fear, the fear of failure, the unknown, or even success. He maintains that only about 4 to 5 percent of the things we fear actually come to pass. Actually, we shouldn't fear failure because without failure at some point, we will never get to success. He wants us to be able to fail as many as seven times before giving up on what we feel we are called to do.

His third "Thing" that successful people do relates to "bringing other along with you" on your upward quest. He talks about time with family, including boardgames and family walks. The two things that our family did to remain in sync was a weekly family meeting and a yearly family vacation. Working with people is very important, but so is play and togetherness.

John's teaching method is: (1) I do it, (2) I show you how to do it, (3) you show me how to do it, and (4) you do it. Most of the sages speak about self-growth and development, but John C. Maxwell has more writing and books about how to be a leader and developer of others than most of the other sages.

AWARENESS
THE FOUR AGREEMENTS
DON MIGUEL RUIZ

"The first step toward personal freedom is awareness. We need to be aware that we are not free in order to be free."

"Imagine living your life without fear of expressing your dreams. You know what you want, what you don't want, and when you want it. You are free to change your life the way you really want to. You are not afraid to ask for what you need, to say yes or no to anything or anyone."

In 1978, my parents bought a condo in Venice, Florida, and moved there from the Cleveland, Ohio, suburbs. From that time on, my wife and I would take our children down for a week in the sun during their spring break from school every March or April. It was always a break from reading professional literature and newspapers, which was my home routine, and I frequented a newsstand/bookstore on my trips to Venice to pick up some "lighter" reading fare while on the beach or in the condo during my vacation week.

On this day, there was a small book that was not in the rack but lying out on the counter as if someone had either left it there by mistake or decided not to purchase it. The size of the book (small) more than the title (*The Four Agreements*) piqued my interest, and I bought it without expecting to be personally edified by whatever the agreements were.

Do I believe in coincidences? Yes, I still believe that coincidences occur, but I also believe that many things that appear as coincidences may be orchestrated from the Universe or a Higher Power in the vernacular of Al-Anon and AA. Today, I truly believe that this little book was left out on the counter for me to see for a reason because the wisdom in this little book has changed my life as much as any book, author, or sage that I will refer to.

Don Miguel Ruiz is a Toltec descendant from Central Mexico. The Toltecs more than any other native Mexican Americans were known as "women and men of great wisdom." Imparting this wisdom is his calling and he has written a number of books on Toltec philosophy, as has his son. Even though he is from an ancient Indian community far removed from European religion, he professes that "Everything is a manifestation of God." Chalk that up to another sage who professes a God of the Universe or a God of their understanding who is in control and has created the world as we know it. So far in this report on the sages that I have read, only Lao-Tzu doesn't specifically dwell on God, although Dr. Dyer definitely talks about "Spirit" and the Creator of the Universe.

According to Miguel Ruiz, all of our problems in this world begin with "Domestication." From the time we are born, we are taught rules and concepts that we carry throughout our lives, whether they are true or not and whether they are helpful or not. These teachings or AGREEMENTS are passed on to us by our parents, teachers, mentors, siblings, friends, and today—social media! We have decided to AGREE that this is the way things are, and as we age we are more closed to the concept of AGEEMENTS that are more helpful to a rewarding life. We also "auto domesticate"! In other words, we tell ourselves concepts that should be followed and truths that may not be really true.

In our learning process, these concepts and laws become our "Book of Life" even if they are wrong. Don Miguel estimates that 95 percent are actually lies! He postulates (and I agree with him) that the motivating thing behind most of the agreements we have accepted is FEAR. He feels human society is ruled by fear. Fear of others, fear of outcomes, fear of things in the future and even fear of being ourselves. In the Course on Miracles, it is postulated that there are only two feelings: Love and Fear. All of the good thoughts, feelings, emotions come from Love and the bad come from Fear. Anger comes from fear as does hate, jealousy, envy, greed, and other unsavory postures. Love promotes kindness, acceptance, happiness, joy, and positivity. Agreements based on fear deplete our energy and those based on love actually create energy.

So since our learned agreements have been so destructive, Don Miguel Ruiz wants us to create some new agreements that will make our lives and the lives of others better. I'm sure there are more than four agreements that will create the "Heaven on earth" that he talks about, but he does not want to overwhelm the reader so he puts forth the four that he feels are most important and lifechanging.

THE FOUR AGREEMENTS:

"Be Impeccable With Your Word."

According to Miguel, this is the most important of the four. Every word we say or write has an effect. The "Message" version of the Bible quotes Jesus as telling his disciples that "words can kill." The words we say or write can lift up or tear down. In 1938, Hitler used words to create a war and kill millions of people. In a personal example, my daughter once told a relative that she wanted to be a doctor. "You barely got out of high school, what makes you think you have a chance to be a doctor?" Of course, because of this WORD she never pursued medicine, although she did become a practical nurse. Gossip, sarcasm, and negativity are misuses of the impeccability of our word. Impeccable means "without sin." The biggest sin is actually self-rejection. We "talk" to ourselves all the time. Are those words or thoughts building us up or tearing us down? Like others we have referenced, Don Miguel believes we need daily affirmation to create positivity in our lives.

"Don't Take Anything Personally."

We do this when we think everything is about "ME." In the Al-Anon program we have a slogan that proclaims: "What other people think about me is none of my business." What people do or say speaks everything about them and not you. We also have a slogan that we call the "Q-TIP," which is just another way of saying Miguel's second agreement: "Quit – Taking It Personally"! Many people who take things personally are "people pleasers." Afraid of rejection or the wrath of others, (we) people pleasers react to the mood of others to make sure they are still in our corner and will not become our antagonists. If they are not pleased, we are convinced it is something we have done or not done. Again, there is that FEAR that pervades almost everything that is negative. Don Miguel, along with the Al-Anon program, teaches us that we should ASK for what we need or want and that it is alright to say NO. Jesus tells us to let our "Yes be Yes and our No be No." Because I am a people pleaser (due to agreements in my upbringing), I created my own slogan: "Don't take everything seriously, or anything personally." It may be necessary to take some things seriously but NONE personally.

"Don't Make Assumptions."

This third agreement is all about communication, which is not my long suit. The two tenets of communication that I lack are listening skills and questioning skills. Actually, I am pretty good at asking questions on topics that are not deep and threatening. Asking how someone feels about a delicate topic is a definite problem for me (there is that FEAR again—fear of rejection, fear of anger or repercussion). But how are we to know what others are thinking or how they feel if we don't ask? That reminds me of the story about the "Trip to Albuquerque." The wife asks her husband if he would like to go to Albuquerque today because she thinks he wants to go. He responds that he would because he surmises that she wants to go or she wouldn't have asked. When they get to Albuquerque, they discover over an argument that neither one wanted to go and the day was not only wasted but ruined. The TRUTH will set you free.

"Always Do Your Best."

Living out the three agreements before this last one in the BEST possible way fulfills this agreement. We may not always be impeccable with our word or take nothing personally or resist making assumptions. But when we do our best, we will always keep these principles in the forefront of our mind and carry them out to the best of our ability on that particular day. This is where AWARENESS comes in. If we keep aware of the best agreements, we are more likely to practice them. This fourth agreement is an ACTION agreement. Again, to combat fear we need to take risks and act on the things that will elevate our lives and those around us. In the Al-Anon program, we have the "3 A's." They are AWARENESS, ACCEPTANCE, and ACTION. A counselor once told me never to use the words "always" or "never." But if we are impeccable with our word and say we will always do our best, it is much more likely to be carried out.

SPIRITUALITY
HOW TO KNOW GOD
DEEPAK CHOPRA

"There is a God of pure being, one who doesn't think but just is. We need him because without a source, our existence has no foundation at all."

"I believe that life events do not unfold randomly; our materialistic worldview may insist that they do, but all of us have reflected on turning points in our lives and seen, sometimes with bafflement or wonder, that lessons came our way at exactly the time we needed them."

Over many years, I have picked up books, tapes and CDs by Dr. Deepak Chopra, a medical doctor with training in India and the United States. He is the consummate amalgamation of scientist, healer, mystic, and spiritual teacher. His writings and teachings are what I would call "heavy." The heaviness comes from his scientific concepts like the use of quantum physics to explain the existence of spiritual entities. Deepak talks about "space-time" realities and hopes the reader will be able to equate molecular mechanics with the principles of the existence and workings of a God who is in the "gap" between thoughts and chemical transmissions.

My most prominent sage over the years has been Wayne Dyer, as I referenced in my comments on his book relating to the Tao. Many of the authors I have and will discuss were introduced to me by Wayne either by direct reference or by presenting joint programs with other sages who later influenced me. Deepak Chopra was one of those influencers I first heard on a tape or CD in a joint program with Wayne Dyer. His soothing voice with a slight Indian dialect was easy to listen to, but his quantum principles and explanations were a little harder to understand and relate to. But hey, if Wayne liked him, I was in as well!

The main reason I liked the writings of Dr. Chopra was that here was a man from an Eastern culture and philosophy who had a spiritual desire and understanding that matched mine. As a scientist and doctor (as am I, although an orthodontist, not a physician), he believes that God is another name for "infinite intelligence" and that arguments against God are based on "facts," but God is deeper than the materialistic world or the world of known "facts."

Once again, this is the eleventh sage studied on my spiritual quest out of the thirty that we will feature, and all eleven have a definite belief in a Higher Power, Spirit, or God as creator and manager of the universe. Lao Tzu did not specifically mention this but the book on the Tao was authored by Wayne Dyer, who became more spiritually aware every year and made numerous references to God.

As a scientist, Deepak Chopra feels that science and religion are not opposites but just different ways of decoding the universe. God's "secrets" are ecstasy, love, grace, and mystery, and he feels that God is not a choice but a necessity! Since the title of this book is "How to Know God," Deepak lists the SEVEN STAGES of spiritual maturity or spiritual growth and how we act and think and relate to our Higher Power in each of those seven stages. The most immature believer is in the first stage, and as we truly seek a closer understanding and relationship with God we move from stage one to stage seven. This takes understanding and the development of a spiritual program that includes prayer and meditation. Most of us journey from Stage One to possibly Stage Four and often regress at times, but the committed seeker can rise as high as they want if totally committed.

In Stage One, the God of your understanding is one of FEAR. You really do not have a close relationship with God even though you believe He or She exists, and your response is one of fight or flight. Many religions in the Western world know that their parishioners do not have a concept of an approachable and loving God, so they use fear to keep them faithful. Fear of God's retribution if you sin, fear of losing God if you don't attend Mass every week are common occurrences in many religions. Deepak feels that Stage One is the most social of the stages and where one learns to be responsible and caring.

Stage Two consists of believers who see God as one who makes laws and rules. Their response to this God is REACTIVE. This means they believe that performance and accomplishments will get them on a higher plane, and they are more ego-driven and self-centered. Winning and succeeding is what will get them rewards, along with God's love and promotion. The spiritual seeker progresses from Stage One to Stage Two. Often this progression is just the result of a little more maturity rather than a closer union with God or a Spiritual Being. In this stage, the individual may worship money or power and even feel God is not necessary. The theme of Stage Two is that "winning is next to Godliness." Despite its external rewards, this stage is the birth of guilt!

Stage Three is where we see the true nature of spiritual growth start to manifest. In this stage we find the RESTFUL AWARENESS response and the individual becomes calmer and more centered. The overbearing, overcontrolling individual in Stage Two can move into a quieter questioning of the nature of God and a more realistic belief that "God is in charge and I'm not." In this stage we have more reflection and bold action. The believer becomes more accepting and much less reactive and managing. In Stage Three believers are inner-directed and focus on silence. An inner-directed person is free of the need for approval. Deepak quotes Jesus as talking about believers being "in the world but not of the world." This level of detachment allows the person in Stage Three to be both detached and engaged.

Stage Four is where we now see ourselves as growing and evolving. The God in this stage is one of the INTUITIVE RESPONSE. In this stage, prayer and meditation are bringing us closer to our Higher Power and we see a clearer plan for the universe as well as our place in it. God in this stage encourages us to reach our highest potential and shows us our purpose in this life. Just as Stage Three sees the birth of a peaceful God, Stage Four sees the birth of a wise God. The God of Stage Four enters one's life only after you make friends with the subconscious. This stage is the first stage that can be seen as "female" oriented. Intuition and the unconscious is generally seen as more of a female characteristic in contrast to the masculine power of reason.

Every stage of inner growth contains more freedom than the stage preceding it. In Stage Five, our creative abilities to fulfill our deepening understanding and relationship with God come out. God inspires us to explore and discover in this CREATIVE RESPONSE. Now we clearly see that "thoughts are things" and you have the ability to "manifest" or create the things that you want in your life. One's imagination and thought process is all-important and one begins to see the hand of God in many of life's normal occurrences. A person in this stage has a strong desire to know and carry out the will of God, but no matter what is achieved there is a strong feeling of gratitude and being blessed by God.

Stage Six is probably as high or as close to God as one can go. Here we have VISIONARY RESPONSE, where advanced spiritual beings can create miracles and bring about healing and advanced wisdom. In this advanced stage it is no longer necessary to seek God, just as we do not have to seek gravity. God is inescapable and constant. This is the stage of overwhelming love and the use of that love to serve other people regardless of the stage of spirituality they are in. You may not know the reason that God created certain events in your life, but you know that it is routinely occurring. Most of our well-known spiritual workers and teachers are in this stage, people like Gandhi, Mandela, the Dalai Lama, Mother Teresa, and others who have spread universal love, healing, and guidance across the globe.

The last or Seventh Stage is the top level where the individual is so free of attachment that if asked who they are, the answer would be "I am." Here you do not even think about time and have no desire to pursue anything. This stage brings the ultimate form of empathy and humility. If we look at three of the major religions in the world, one might consider Jesus Christ, the Buddha, and Mohammed to be representative of this stage. It is pure love, pure wisdom, timeless and all-encompassing. One can go no higher without being God Himself.

When I read Deepak's description of the seven stages of spiritual growth or the "stairsteps to spiritual awakening," I couldn't help but think of the AA and Al-Anon Twelve-Step Program. The "Twelve Steps" have the same purpose as Deepak's Seven Stages. In the program, we are seeking a "Spiritual Awakening" and the Steps are sequential efforts to move up the ladder from no relationship with a God of our understanding to the awakening, which gives us a knowing that God is in charge and it is only through a strong belief and trust in God or a Higher Power that we can achieve Serenity and a redeeming existence. Step Eleven is where we use continuous "prayer and meditation to improve our conscious contact with God, praying only for his will for us and the power to carry it out." And the final step states that "Having had a Spiritual Awakening as a result of these (12) Steps, we carry this message to others and practice these principles in all our affairs." Like Deepak's Stages, the Steps must be taken in order to achieve this awakening. There is no jumping over steps to get the awakening we all desire. Once we know that God is in control, we can "Let Go and Let God" and live a life of love, peace, and understanding.

When one takes a look at people in our country today, it is fairly easy to see where most of us reside on the ladder to Stage Seven. My guess is that a majority of the population in the United States is in Stage One. They know there is a God but have no relationship or confidence in Him or Her, although they may offer a hasty prayer in times of trouble as a last resort. Their lives are based on worry, fear, anger, and "making it through the day" or looking forward to the weekend or retirement. They are easily controlled and swayed by social media, politicians with conspiracy theories, and TV, movies, and other fantasies. They are in Stage One because they have no desire to climb the ladder to a higher stage.

The next large segment of our populace is in Stage Two. These are people who were fortunate enough to be born into families with a little higher standard of living and income and can afford advanced education and training. More is naturally expected of this group, and they become high earners, professional athletes, and corporate heads. Obviously, politicians all fall into this category as well. In this country, these people are mostly male and white. The capitalistic system has energized these people to produce and rule. Power and money become more of a God than the real Higher Power. They usually go to church and "praise the Lord" because they are on top and might even give God a little credit for their success. Many of these people will use their money and position to lift up others and show the love and mercy of God and hopefully these outreaches will continue and get stronger.

My uneducated guess is that only a small percentage of people in the United States get higher than the first two stages. My guess would be 15 to 20 percent. Once I began to "work" the Al-Anon program and got involved in the Twelve Steps I was able to move to Stage Three, according to Deepak Chopra, in that I was more centered and calmer although prone to occasional "awfulizing" and overreaction to adverse occurrences. My tendency toward being an "approval addict" occasionally sent me tumbling all the way back into Stage One! Stage Three taught me that "What other people think about me is none of my business." I can even say that there are times where I venture into Stage Four and even touch the outskirts of Stage Five. I see things that

God has done in my behalf on a regular basis and my prayer and meditation life is very consistent, as is my Al-Anon meeting attendance and service work.

Deepak talks about the importance of "Awareness" of the presence of God around us on a daily moment-to-moment basis and that our Soul is found in the "light" of God. As we climb the spiritual ladder, whether using Deepak's Seven Stages or Bill Wilson's Twelve Steps, we not only see the light but we also become the "light" to carry to others out of love and service. As Jesus said on the Mount, "You wouldn't hide your light under a bushel basket." Let it shine for the sake of your part of the world.

Dr. Chopra ends his search to know God by listing ten "ground rules" for creating the "intention" of becoming more spiritually astute. The ones I relate to the most are: (1) See yourself in the light, (2) See everyone else in the light, (3) Learn to forgive yourself (and others), (4) Learn to let go! (and let God), (5) Revere what is holy, (6) Allow God to take over, and (7) Embrace the unknown.

PRESENCE
THE POWER OF NOW
ECKHART TOLLE

"The pain that you create now is always some form of nonacceptance, some form of unconscious resistance to what is."

"Realize deeply that the present moment is all you ever have. Make the NOW the primary focus of your life."

Before I read *The Power of Now*, I listened to tapes and CDs of Eckhart's spiritual concepts and theories. Like Deepak Chopra, I believe I first heard about his teachings and philosophy from Dr. Wayne Dyer, who was my chief sage in the eighties and nineties. One CD or podcast had both Dr. Dyer and Eckhart on "stage" together with Dr. Dyer claiming he was the "number-two spiritual guru" as opposed to Eckhart being the "number-one" that people listened to. After reading and listening to Eckhart, I'm sure he was uncomfortable with any type of personal ranking or hierarchy. Dr. Dyer began his teachings in the seventies with a bit of an ego, and even in the later years some of this still remained even though he conceded that Eckhart was now the more referenced and listened to for spiritual teaching.

The CDs that Eckhart Tolle first created allowed the listener to hear his soft, soothing voice, which demonstrated his calm and quiet presence. The listener was also rewarded with his cute, impish sense of humor and delightful laugh in which he seemed to be breathing in rather than breathing out. He was originally from Germany but learned his English in Great Britain, so he had a barely perceptible German/British accent. Maybe some of it was Canadian because when he moved to North America, he took up residence and teaching in Vancouver, British Columbia.

Both Deepak Chopra and Eckhart Tolle are not only advanced spiritual teachers, but both have brilliant minds and similar concepts to achieve the "peace that passes all understanding" and the enlightenment that can bring us closer to Spirit or God. Deepak wants us to get closer to God by a seven-step process and Eckhart wants that to happen by being totally accepting and enjoying the NOW. Both of these non-American sages quote Jesus, Buddha, and other spiritual teachers, as well as writings such as *The Course in Miracles*. On the cover of *The Power of Now*, Deepak Chopra promotes the Eckhart book with the quote "One of the best books to come along in years. Every sentence rings with truth and power."

Some of our previous authors have focused on the power of "thoughts" and "thinking." One says "a man is as he thinketh" and "thoughts are things." Some have professed that positive thinking and "visualization" is what creates the success we are out to achieve. In this book, Eckhart Tolle also states that thoughts are powerful but not that they are keys to success but that they are the cause of affliction and disease! The mind (thoughts) are what cause us problems. If we live in the NOW or the present moment, the mind and its incessant thinking are removed and we have peace. He postulates that unless you stay in the present moment, you will continue to be run by your mind. This may be fueled by the one basic emotion that underlies the mind-identified state of unconsciousness or FEAR.

Fear is caused by living in or for the future. We worry about the economy, World War III, the stock market, disease, age, disability, and this steals the joy of what is happening NOW.

In order to have the peace and joy that we deserve, we have to learn to ACCEPT WHAT IS and not use the mind to think about what may happen or even what has happened a few minutes ago. We find almost all the other sages cautioning that fear is a primary agent to destroy not only the joy in life but also relationships and a connection to God. In the Al-Anon program, we are taught to "Turn our life and our will over to God" and thus we can move forward with minimal fear depending on the degree that we trust God or our Higher Power in our lives.

In *The Power of Now*, Eckhart quotes Jesus more than any other spiritual teacher even though he does not seem to be a professed Christian. In discussing fear of the future in regards to worry, he quotes Jesus teaching from Philippians 4-6: "Do not be anxious or worried about anything, but in every situation by prayer and petition, continue to make your request known to God." And then again from the "Sermon on the Mount" in Matthew: "Consider the lilies (flowers), they neither toil nor spin yet your father feeds them. Can any of you by worrying add a single moment to your lifetime?"

The opposite of living in the future is dredging up things in the past. When we do this, we tend to live with guilt, regret, and resentment. Even the positive things in the past cause us to fantasize rather than attend to our life as it is happening NOW. In the Al-Anon program, we have a saying or slogan: "It's alright to look back, but don't stare." Too much depression and grief come from reliving what has occurred, which we cannot change. We only "look back" as a lesson about what to do or not do when the next similar situation occurs.

My sponsor in Al-Anon is also in the AA program and sponsors many men in that recovery group. When he has them take the Fourth Step (a searching and fearless moral inventory), he gives them a sheet of paper with two columns on it. The first column is entitled FEAR and they are to list all the fears that are causing them to take drugs and have less than an optimum life. In the second column is the word RESENTMENT. The alcoholic then lists all the things that cause him or her to resent others or life in general. It is not a coincidence that FEAR of the future and RESENTMENT of the past are huge triggers for the addict and living in the present or the NOW would eliminate both of those defects of character.

When we live in and for the present moment, we must learn to ACCEPT life as it is or has happened. This requires us to be nonresistant and nonjudgmental. Eckhart calls this total SURRENDER to what is. The Al-Anon slogan that I made up is "Accept, Surrender, Let Go, Let God." This turning all things over to a Higher Power emphasizes my lack of control over what happens and puts the end result in a power greater than myself. This creates HUMILITY and the ability to withstand whatever has occurred in the NOW.

One of my "attitude heroes" is a good friend who graduated from dental school with me in the 60s. Whenever anything happens unexpectedly and is somewhat negative, he just laughs and says: "Isn't that interesting." When something negative occurs in my life, I am more prone to get upset and shout mild to moderate swear words. The effects of the event also last much longer than the gentle acceptance and laughter of my colleague.

ACCEPTANCE is really the basic tenant of the Al-Anon and AA program. The Serenity Prayer tells us that serenity or peace of mind comes from acceptance of the things we cannot change. Things that occur in the NOW cannot be changed. They have happened and just are. The only thing we can do is accept them. In his book, Tolle professes that after acceptance comes action. Action is always better than no action. And of course, that action will occur in the present. He states that complaining about something is equal to nonacceptance to what is. Again, this teaching is emphasized in Al-Anon's "three A's"—Awareness, Acceptance, and Action. Be aware of what is, accept it, and decide what (if anything) to do about it!

When my youngest son was a teenager, my wife and I took him with us to Montana for an orthodontic convention. Since we were in the mountains, I talked him into going mountain biking with me down one of the slopes (in the summertime). We took the chair lift to the top and after yelling "Follow me!" I took both of us the wrong way and we wound up on the other side of the mountain, at least ten miles from our hotel. My son was livid, telling me, "I told you this was the wrong way!" The incessant complaining and chastising continued for a long time. For me, this was a teaching experience. Now that we were here, how and why we got here was of little concern. The only question was what we were going to do about it. There was a golf course a few hundred yards away, and I saw a man working on a golf cart in a garage next to the course. While my son continued to berate me, I walked over to the man, told him of our plight, and he said: "Put your bikes in my van, I have to make a delivery on the other side of the mountain in the same center where you rented your bikes." Of course, I thought this would be a great learning experience for my young son—it's not what happens to you, it's how you respond to what happened that is important. I'm not sure that he really was teachable at that time in his life because he continued to berate me on the short trip in the van!

EGO in the Al-Anon program stands for "Edging God Out." Eckhart Tolle refers to the EGO all throughout his book. The EGO needs problems as well as worries and resentments to survive. There must be conflict and there also must be enemies. The EGO needs power, money, relationships, and recognition. The EGO's power over others is weakness disguised as strength. Like Chopra and other authors we have discussed, enlightenment is described as the "light" that Jesus referred to when he said his disciples were to be the "light and the salt of the earth." When the EGO is in control, it means the "light" is too painful for someone choosing darkness.

One of the original theories advanced by Eckhart is the presence of the "Pain-body." Anger and negativity come from this "body" in a person due to past painful events in their lives or their upbringing. Because of this, when events happen that trigger this "body" the individual can become more oppositional and easily lose the "peace that passes all understanding" as referenced in the Bible.

When we live in the NOW, there is no "time" and no "waiting." Of course, we need chronological clock time, but in the spiritual universe everything happens NOW so time is not a factor. Much of my life has been involved with "waiting." How many more months till my vacation or my shoulder surgery? Sometimes waiting is in fear of an adverse event and sometimes it is in joyful anticipation of a positive event. At the present time, I am waiting for next summer to get a dog and have been waiting for a romantic relationship for the past five years! In thinking obsessively on these things, I am forgetting to enjoy and live in the only time I have on this earth, the NOW.

BOLDNESS
AWAKEN THE GIANT WITHIN
TONY ROBBINS

"It is in your moments of decision that your destiny is shaped."

"Everything you and I do; we do either out of our need to avoid pain or our desire to gain pleasure."

Every morning, I read the page for the day in the "Daily Word" as a part of my daily inspirational and spiritual practice, along with my three Al-Anon daily readers, the Bible, and another daily religious book, as well as meditating for twenty minutes using the *Calm* app on my phone. The reading in the Daily Word this morning started with a quote, which read: "I live from my divine spirit with zeal and excitement!" This very aptly reminds me of Tony Robbins' persona and philosophy of life. The other words that define him for me are passionate and outrageous.

Like many of the other sages profiled before Robbins, I never read any of his books but became familiar with his teaching and opinions through 8-track tapes back in the 90s. The book that I am referring to in this profile is called *Awaken the Giant Within*, and in order to comment on him more fully I did read it over the last month and recalled some of the passion and enthusiasm that he also portrayed in his tapes. His audio recordings featured a very "gravelly" type voice, not exactly like he had marbles in his mouth but like he needed to clear his throat before moving on. I was impressed and drawn in by his apparent excitement and positive delivery and energy. The book I chose to feature was published in 1991, but the principles and teachings may be more important today than at the end of the 20th century.

The thing I remember the most from Tony's tapes in the 80s and 90s was a story about his community outreach at Thanksgiving. He purchased a large amount of turkeys and then took them to street corners in New York City, along with others from his company or family. When cars stopped for red lights or just to see what he was doing on the street corner, he would offer them a Thanksgiving turkey! That lesson motivated me to act similarly in my community, and at the time my two youngest children were preteens. I thought I could serve people at Thanksgiving and provide a lesson for them, so I acted on the Robbin's Thanksgiving turkey delivery.

The city of Canton had a homeless shelter for four families who had lost their homes due to finances, fires, or abandonment. I would take my wife and two children shopping for about $100 worth of groceries for each family, along with the turkeys and Thanksgiving food items, and then deliver it to the shelter several weeks before Thanksgiving. We did this until my two children started at schools out of the area and then I continued doing it with my St. Paul's Sunday School class for the next ten or fifteen years, until my religious education "career" ended. Tony Robbins' altruism extended beyond Thanksgiving as well since he developed the habit or giving money to people in airports who appeared to be in need.

In his book, Tony Robbins refers to and quotes some of the other sages we have discussed, primarily Jim Rohn and Wayne Dyer. I would put his writings in the same vein as Jim Rohn in that he is trying to instill enthusiasm for personal growth and achievement for the reader. The message is that "you are what you DECIDE you are." You have the energy and power to become anything you want to be if you are willing to engage in it and do the action and work it takes. Like Jim Rohn there is a small reference to spiritual growth, but the emphasis is on personal development that can be accomplished if you follow the precepts outlined in his books and seminars and have the excitement and passion that he displays as a necessary behavior. There is a little "ego"-driven emphasis that is demonstrated that reminds me of Wayne Dyer's earlier writings. Wayne became more spiritual as his career evolved and Tony Robbins touches on spirituality but not as a primary outreach. In mentioning the need for patience in personal development, Tony does quote that "God's delays are not God's denials."

The basis for *Awaken the Giant Within*, as well as the tapes of the 80s that I heard, all come down to two words: "Pleasure" and "Pain." All human behavior is centered around these two feelings. People are motivated to do things that bring them pleasure and motivated to avoid things that bring them pain. Tony Robbins' biggest revelation was that avoiding pain was a bigger motivator than trying to gain pleasure. FEAR (as we mentioned in past pages) is a huge motivator in preventing people from doing what will advance their lives and allow then to "awaken the giant within." We may find pleasure in a trip to France but decide that traveling six hours in a plane with masks or people with COVID cancels the idea that this is a good move. We believe that parachuting would be exhilarating but the thought of injury or even death motivates us to disregard such an activity. Tony Robbins even discusses Donald Trump in this vein, saying that for Donald coming in second is so painful that he was motivated to achieve in order to avoid this painful possibility. Remember, this was written in the past century and thirty years later, former President Trump refuses to accept "coming in second" and must believe the election was corrupt in order to avoid the pain of losing.

Tony uses the CANI principle for his motivational discourse. This stands for "Constant And Never-ending Improvement." The reader must wake up each day and make a pledge to move their goals, principles, and life in a constant upward and onward direction. At the end of the day, they must ask themselves the important QUESTIONS: (1) What did I learn today? (2) What did I give to others today? and (3) What have I done that added to or uplifted the quality of my life today? We are to continuously ask ourselves those and other questions that will allow us to learn and elevate us over what we were the day before.

The Serenity Prayer tells us that we need "courage to change the things we can." This basically means ourselves, the only thing we have control over. Tony preaches the need for an upward change but maintains that positive change only works with the proper reinforcement. He developed a program called Neuro-Associative Conditioning (NAC), which deals with the importance of FOCUS and URGENCY if we are to change positively and maintain what we have gained. His focus is on the "top of the mountain," not on either looking back down the mountain or lamenting where we are. As a senior citizen, I truly appreciate one of his quotes in this vein: "Getting old is not age, it's a lack of movement!" I try to live this philosophy every day, although I might add to it. Getting old is a lack of having something to do that makes your life useful and worthwhile.

Like Jim Rohn and many sages we have visited, Tony Robbins emphasizes the importance of GOALS. Like others have preached, the goals must be written and constantly followed. There must be a PLAN in place for achieving your goals and checking progress daily. One of his goals is daily READING. He reads voraciously and much of the wisdom he imparts is from a myriad of other sources that he had read. And his reading interest is not all motivational material but scientific, historical, and even fictional. The word most important in goal achievement is persistence, a daily conscious effort to achieve what you said you would.

Two categories that Robbins feels are important are WORDS and EMO-TIONS. Like Don Miguel Ruiz said in *The Four Agreements*, you must be "impeccable with your word." For Tony, that means using only affirmative words in your speech about you and others. Instead of saying "I am so distressed," try saying "I am so peeved" or some other silly word that does not take you to a negative place. Try to cultivate positive emotional states and eliminate the negative. An example would be that the result of an event left you "frustrated" rather than "disappointed." It may only be semantics, but your brain wiring will react better to a more upbeat description of what is going on in your life on a moment-to-moment basis. Again, Tony uses a quote from Donald Trump (in the 80s), in which he states that "Life is a TEST." In other words, in life you either win or lose. Contrast that to Forrest Gump saying that "Life is like a box of chocolates."

Besides WORDS and EMOTIONS, there are three categories that Tony Robbins feels you have to understand in order to have a successful life. The first is VALUES. He lists about ten or twelve values that he wants us to choose from. I chose Love, Intimacy, and Health over Power, Passion, and Security, although I am sure that Tony is more in the Power and Passion category than I would ever be. He does mention that these values can change during one's lifetime, so you must continually decide what is most important to you.

The second important category is RULES. In the Al-Anon program, we would call this BOUNDARIES rather than rules. Again, if we look at the third of the "Four Agreements," we are not to "assume" another person's rules. We need to constantly ask questions of others before we behave toward them in an unacceptable or harmful manner.

The third category is IDENTITY. We are who we say we are. We are not our profession or our living status. We must create powerful acknowledgment that we are "children of God" (mine, not Tony's quote). We are also who we BELIEVE we are. We can act our way into better thinking and elevate our identity in our own eyes, which will in turn elevate it in the eyes of the people we are involved with.

Near the end of this nearly 500-page book, Tony has a weekly program with practical ideas for each day of a seven-day week, working on one facet of positive, passionate living. On day one he gives lessons on developing EMPOWERING EMOTIONS. Day two focuses on HEALTH AND ENERGY. Day three focuses on developing sound RELATIONSHIPS. Day four is teaching you to get your FINANCES IN ORDER. Day five has suggestions on developing a proper CODE OF CONDUCT. Day six features on the proper use of TIME and as a final reference to the Bible, day seven is a day of REST!

Also, near the back of the book Tony encourages us to get involved in improving the world and mentions his efforts in water conservation, global warming (yes, back in the 80s!), world hunger and a lot of other outreaches in which he is using his energy, passion, money, and time in to make a difference. His many seminars also encourage participants to get involved in at least one ministry that will make a change for the better in the world we live in. My issues are LOCAL HUNGER and NATIONAL GUN CONTROL. I have volunteered at a local soup kitchen with my practice, my religious education class, and individually and support that local outreach. I also donate to several local food banks monthly. My gun-control efforts have been mainly writing letters to politicians about stricter gun laws that, to date, have not made a difference. Tony would agree that the efforts and intentions are more important than the results.

Tony makes a statement along with many other sages that is hard for me to buy into. The quote that "Everything Happens for a Reason" is hard to believe. I just lost one of my two best friends to a car accident caused by a drunk driver. He was the kindest, gentlest person on earth and was helping a huge number of newcomers in the Al-Anon program. I will never be able to believe there was a reason for him not to continue his outreach and mission on this earth. Besides this concept, it is difficult to generate the constant action and achievement mindset that Tony has at my current stage in life. The emphasis on personal growth is most valuable for someone in their twenties, although it is good to be reminded that we are never too old to make a difference. People at my stage in life can benefit more from Tony Robbins' altruism example because we might have more time and finances to give back to our local community, our country, and the world in general.

LEARNING
THE WAY OF THE PEACEFUL WARRIOR
DAN MILLMAN

"The secret of happiness, you see, is not found in seeking more, but in developing the capacity to enjoy less."

"There are no ordinary moments!"

As the last quote above indicates, this narrative semi-fiction story put together by Dan Millman professes that every moment in life is precious. As several of the sages we have already investigated, this author suggests that we value the present moment because it is all we have, and we must fully enjoy the sights and sounds of each life experience as it happens. Keep your eyes and ears open at all times and look for the richness of the myriad experiences of this life. Al-Anon slogans that would speak to this are "Listen and Learn" and "Keep an Open Mind."

Dan Millman is a gymnast and spiritual teacher who has written several books that speak to developing spiritual and physical concepts of living. The books are fiction "stories" about Dan's encounter with an elderly gas station attendant who seems to have dynamic physical and mental attributes. The fictional Dan calls this mentor "Socrates," and the principles that he teaches Dan are the basis of the story and the lessons that Dan Millman wants to get across to the reader. The story parallels Dan's own life in terms of his college attendance, gymnastic endeavors, living situations in California, Ohio, and other locations. The principles he teaches through the relationship with "Socrates" and other fictional teachers make the reading of a self-improvement book much easier and more fun.

After reading his short story in the mid-eighties, I also listened to several of his 8-track tapes on my car stereo. He reminds me of Tony Robbins in that he is young and passionate and has a very proactive idea about moving constantly forward both physically and spiritually. The very title of his book, which includes the word "Warrior," indicates that we need to advance physically through life's obstacles and challenges with the mind of a strong warrior albeit a peaceful one instead of one bent on harming others or ourselves with abusive conduct.

The young collegiate Dan of the book learns many lessons from his newfound mentor, Socrates. Since I am quite a bit beyond college age, I can easily look back and see the many mentors in my life. During my collegiate years at Allegheny College, a counselor named Dr. Wharton gave me a batch of tests that changed me from a failing pre-law student to a successful biology, predent major. He was no Socrates but he changed my life, as I would have been a terrible lawyer. In my dental internship in Pittsburgh, Dr. Arnie Rosenthal invited me down to his office and after I told him I wanted be an orthodontist like him, he wrote letters of recommendations to many schools.

When I joined my orthodontic partner, Dr. Harry Osborne, in North Canton, he become my professional mentor. He was board certified, so I pushed forward toward board certification because he was the standard. He was the president of our local dental society, so I knew I had to become president as well for our practice to flourish and be recognized among our dental peers. Harry introduced me to Mr. Bud Schulman, who became my business mentor. Because of Bud, I made many sound practice and real estate decisions and learned a lot from a study group he organized back in the early eighties.

When I joined Al-Anon in the mid-seventies, the women of the Louisville meeting were my mentors and Carol R. was my first sponsor and allowed me to take my first fifth Step and begin on the way to completing all 12 Steps of the program. Today, I am on my third sponsor (mentor) and Cary and I meet at least once a month to make sure my program is on the right track.

And now, I am a teacher or clinical instructor in two orthodontic departments and am hopefully a mentor to over forty dentists who are hoping to learn the techniques and skills that I used in my orthodontic practice for over forty-six years. As *The Way of the Peaceful Warrior* demonstrates, we all should have mentors in life like Socrates that show us the "Way" and influence our lives positively as we learn and grow spiritually, physically, mentally, and emotionally on a daily basis.

One of the first lessons Socrates teaches Dan is that life requires more than knowledge, it requires INTENSE FEELING and CONSTANT ENERGY. The spiritual warrior acts whereas the fool reacts. The warrior does not blame others or circumstances but takes responsibility for moving forward and progressing in their quest.

Before we are trained as warriors, we spend a lot of time in our mind. As Socrates teaches Dan in his gas station each night, the mind is the source of "your predicament." We spend too much time in our thought processes and the mind is the source of our moods, especially our negative moods. In Al-Anon we have the simple one-word slogan: "Think." But in Millman's book, he indicates that too much thinking gets us into trouble, especially negative thinking. One of my resolutions this year is to eliminate negative thought processes. Often on my drive home from my distant teaching jobs, I think back over the treatment of a patient that wasn't going well and wished I had given the student better instructions on how to handle the faulty treatment. Socrates would have me leave the "faulty treatment plan" at the school the moment I left and not ruminate negatively on "what a lousy instructor I am" and "why couldn't I have told the student to do x instead of y."

Many of our sages speak negatively about anger, but Dan Millman believes that anger is stronger than fear or sorrow. You just need to be able to find the proper use of it and be able to bridle it so no one is hurt by it. Anger can be a catalyst for change that must be made. Change is a law, nothing is constant, but we are in charge of changes that benefit us and the people in our lives.

Since the advice that Socrates gives Dan encompasses physical and spiritual growth and wellbeing, there are some practices that are critical and most are espoused by other growth specialists.

DIET: The Spiritual warrior gets his or her energy from a non-meat, vegetable, nut, and legume protein diet. They avoid sugar, flour, and even coffee! I'm not sure what Socrates finds objectionable about coffee, but I have recently found that I can think better and have more energy with one cup of coffee before the YMCA in the morning. I have one cup of decaffeinated coffee after 8 in the evening. None of my mentors have told me the bad effect of coffee so I will continue that habit but will eliminate meat, most flour, and most sugar.

MEDITATION: Almost 100 percent of spiritual teachers profess the practice of meditation or at least "mindfulness." The practice of breathing slowly and deeply. This gives you both insight and the ability to surrender. If done correctly, it improves the posture and aids in "overcoming the mind."

TAI CHI: Socrates does not go into the Asian art very much, but this helps slow the breathing, gets us out of our mind (thinking), and improves our flexibility and posture.

Besides living in the PRESENT MOMENT, as almost all sages have indicated is a mandatory practice, we have to actively practice NON-RESISTANCE. Millman (or Socrates) would have us be like a palm tree and when resistance comes up we bend with it, not against it. We "row, row, row the boat, gently down the stream" and do not fight the current and go upstream. We have no attachment to any outcome and are able to SURRENDER to what is. The mantra that one uses in any action undertaken is to "JUST DO YOUR BEST, AND LET GOD HANDLE THE REST." This is one of the few references that Dan Millman makes to God or a Higher Power. He does mention in one instance a quote that Jesus made about becoming like a little child to enter the Kingdom of Heaven. In this passage, he calls Jesus "one of the Great Warriors."

Other sages have stated that "there are no coincidences in life" and Dan Millman is in that camp. He professes that there are "no accidents." Everything has a purpose, even if that purpose is a lesson. In discussing previous authors, I have stated my belief that there are accidents. God allows some things to happen and some things to be altered in accordance with his will (and prayers of people). My best friend Rand's death in an auto "accident" was not for a purpose and offered no lesson other than life is fragile and the good die young.

As a spiritual warrior, Dan is taught by Socrates to live the "simple way." Be sure to lower your desires and wants. Stay in the present and be vulnerable and loving. Surrender brings happiness as does living within your means. It amazes me that pro athletes that make 20 million a year hold out for 25 million to make ends meet and then are bankrupt by the age of fifty. People play the lottery when it is over 200 million and they have no chance to win because of the odds but do not play when it is just one million and the odds are much more favorable. The culture says more is better and Socrates says more is the road to strife, heartache, and delusion. At the present time, I only own a five-year-old car. My house belongs to my children, I sold my practice, my house, my condo in Florida, and my office building. I am happier and more financially stable than ever before in my life.

In the last pages of Dan Millman's story, he concludes that "there is no need to search; achievement leads to nowhere." It makes no difference at all, so just be happy now! Love is the only reality of the world because it is all One, you see. And the only laws are paradox, humor, and change. Release your struggles, let go of your mind, throw away your concerns, and relax into the world. No need to resist life; JUST DO YOUR BEST! (one of the "Four Agreements" from Don Miguel Ruiz).

UNDERSTANDING
THE 7 HABITS OF HIGHLY EFFECTIVE PEOPLE STEPHEN R. COVEY

"Each of us tends to think we see things as they are, that we are _objective._ But this is not the case. We see the world, not as it is, but as we are—or as we are conditioned to see it."

"Communication is the most important skill in life."

Stephan Covey may be the most well-rounded sage of them all. He is really defined as a business guru, teaching on leadership and management and working with companies to increase their effectiveness, not just their efficiency. When I think of his teaching and lifestyle, the word that comes to mind is _discipline._ In order for your paradigm to match his, you have to be very focused and disciplined. For your business or life to grow using his "7 Habits," you have to be diligent and committed to the principles he teaches. However, his "habits" and wisdom will also give you a more fulfilling personal life and encompasses a strong spiritual component with a strong belief in God and the wisdom and direction of the Bible.

The college-teacher-turned-business-mentor first wrote in the mid-eighties that there were basically seven habits that you needed to practice in order to be effective in business and life. His premise is that the often-taught "Personality Ethic" must be replaced by a "Principle centered, character-based Ethic." The writers and speakers who were motivational or positive-thinking and attitude-based teachers were focusing on an "outside – in" learning paradigm and his philosophy was the opposite or from an "inside – out" ethic. He uses the formula P/PC, which stands for a balance between P (production) and

PC (production capability). The example is the tale of the farmer who had a goose that laid golden eggs. Because he only got a few eggs each day, he decided to sacrifice the goose to harvest all the eggs faster. Of course, in doing so he killed the producer of the golden eggs. So he lost the balance between production and production capability.

The 7 Habits are broken down into three categories. The first three are called the "Private Victory" habits. In other words, they are habits that you must develop "Independently." You must develop these character traits from within with a strong personal commitment and little outside help. Until these habits are well ingrained in your principle-centered makeup, you cannot move on to the other more advanced categories with others.

PRIVATE VICTORY – Independence

HABIT ONE – BE PROACTIVE

"Get up, Get out, Get it on!" My slogan from the Al-Anon program that addresses this habit is "Just do it and detach from the outcome." Proactivity is driven by proper values, whereas being reactive is driven by feelings. You must take responsibility for moving forward on your values-based commitments. Proactive people make "love" a verb rather than a noun. The ability to achieve happiness is a decision as is love. As Abraham Lincoln postulated, "A person is as happy as they make up their mind to be."

Stephen Covey uses many diagrams and charts in the book, and in this chapter he uses two large concentric circles entitled "Circle of Concern" and an inner "Circle of Influence." We are to move forward on those things or people we can influence and not be attached to the things that concern us but cannot be influenced by us. As the Serenity Prayer states: "God grant me the serenity to accept the things I cannot change; courage to change the things I can (proactivity); and wisdom to know the difference." Proactivity or forward and right-directed action is based on resourcefulness and initiative, and you must have both to be successful. Don't wait for life!

HABIT TWO – BEGIN WITH THE END IN MIND

After I had purchased and read the Covey masterpiece in the eighties, I heard he was coming to Cleveland to give a one-day presentation and I talked a few dentist friends into attending with me. As he walked into the room, he pulled down the screen and projected the image of a large star in the middle. With a pointer he tapped on the star and said, "This is True North! You may recognize it as the North Star but it is your True North. We all have a 'True North' in life, and everyone's is different. Just make sure that you are heading toward your 'True North' every day of your life." In other words, know where you are headed or you will wind up in the wrong place.

Another way that Stephen taught this was the idea that "before you put a ladder up against the wall, make sure you are putting it against the right wall." Why climb a ladder to success that will not take you to the successful result you want to achieve? We need to take an example from professional athletes and "visualize" what we want to accomplish before we do it. Much of the chapter on knowing where you are going in life is devoted to creating a "mission statement": TO LIVE A VALUES-BASED LIFE OF LOVE AND SERVICE TOWARD MY FAMILY, FRIENDS, STUDENTS AND GOD. Okay, I admit this mission statement was spontaneous and hurried and we are taught to take our time and make many revisions before we have our True North statement hammered out. However, when I had a marriage, a young family, and an active practice, I did have a personal, professional, and family mission statement in place. Of course, when you have others involved they have to be in on the creation of the statement of purpose and direction.

HABIT THREE – PUT FIRST THINGS FIRST

Once we know our "True North" and our direct heading, we must prioritize the steps required in getting there. Like almost all the sages we have covered, Stephen Covey emphasized the importance of GOALS in this third habit. The goals must be practical, written, and measurable. Organization is one of Stephen's talents, and in this habit he uses a weekly "planner" to indicate the steps necessary to accomplish the goals we list. In deciding what to put first, we must put relationship and results over time and methods. Even in the private victory habits, we must continue to maintain respect and kindness toward other individuals.

As he does with other habits, diagrams are used to depict the importance of knowing what things to put first. A large square is divided up into four quadrants. The upper-left quadrant is for things that are important and urgent, the upper-right is for things that are important and not urgent. The lower two quadrants are for things not important and urgent, and the lower-right is for things that are not important and not urgent (watching TV, eating a sugary snack, checking the sports results on your phone). It is pointed out that we should really live mostly in "Quadrant Two," working on things that are important but not a crisis.

This third habit involves delegating as much as we can to others, which requires building relationships. Since we know what the most important things are, we can delegate the lesser-important things to others. In this habit, we also establish proper boundaries and learn that the word "NO" is a complete sentence.

PUBLIC VICTORY – Interdependence

HABIT FOUR – THINK WIN/WIN

In this first habit that directly deals with interacting with others, we are introduced to the concept of the "Emotional Bank Account." Instead of dollars, we are depositing either good will or bad will with all people that we relate to. Affirming others by being kind, honest, and committed will add to our emotional bank account with them. Treating them poorly will make withdrawals from that emotional account. We can even add to the account if we apologize sincerely after doing something that causes a withdrawal. People who talk well about people who are not even present are adding to the emotional bank accounts of the people they refer to and the people they are relating to at the time.

In situations where two or more people need to come together for a solution of an issue, there are five possible outcomes. The ideal outcome is "Win/Win." Both parties leave the table feeling that they have "won" and are satisfied and both have enhanced emotional bank accounts. In the "Win/Lose" result, I have won and we are doing it my way in deference to your goals. However, in the opposite or "Lose/Win" ending, I have capitulated to your wishes and have lost, which I am not happy about. There are two other possible results—the compromise, which is a weak "Win/Win," and the NO DEAL, which is really the best solution until a "Win/Win" can be achieved.

People who have a "Scarcity Mentality" tend to have trouble with this habit, whereas those with an "Abundance Mentality" realize that there is always enough for everyone. With this outlook, comparing and competing are often avoided. In a talk I heard Stephen Covey give on an 8-track tape, he maintained that the four evil "C's" were Competing, Comparing, Complaining, and Criticizing. I wholeheartedly agree!

In my marriage, I decided to move out of the house when my wife and I only had "Lose/Lose" confrontations. Of course, she had relapsed into acute alcoholism and was spending money on outside interests that I felt were not warranted. When I would confront her about this, she would become angry and bring up all the indiscretions I had carried out during the last ten years of our marriage. When the session was over, she was extremely angry and I was depressed and defeated. We had both lost. This type of faulty communication led to our divorce.

HABIT FIVE – SEEK FIRST TO UNDERSTAND AND THEN TO BE UNDERSTOOD

Stephen Covey admits that this is not only the most important of the interdependent habits, but it is the hardest for him to comply with. I totally agree!

My wife always told me that I was a poor listener. This did not add to my emotional bank account, but she was right (as she usually was when sober). My mind is usually trying to come up with a response rather than focusing on the actual intent of the speaker. At the Al-Anon meetings I attend we have a topic for the hour session, and I am usually mulling over in my mind what I should or want to say about the topic rather than listening to what others have to say. As a result, I miss much of the wisdom that others impart to the group.

In this habit, we are to repeat what we heard the person say to us to make sure we truly understand what thought they are trying to convey. I can honestly say that I can't ever remember doing that, even after listening to or reading the material on the "7 Habits"! When I was in active orthodontic practice, I would be in my office going over a treatment plan when one of my coworkers would come in with an issue or information. It was extremely hard to put down my paperwork or radiograph and intently focus on them and what they wanted my attention for.

We have a saying in the Al-Anon program, "Practice Lowly Listening," which is the same thing as what the 7 *Habits* book refers to as "Empathic Listening." This means putting everything aside, looking the other person directly in the eye and focusing on every word as well as the context of what they are saying. We are to ask questions that relate to their statements, even if we don't rephrase what we think we heard them say. In the 7 *Habits* book, this is called giving the speaker "Psychological Air." When people know they are being listened to and understood, they immediately feel comfortable and validated. And they feel much more in touch and interconnected with the listener.

HABIT SIX – SYNERGIZE

Life is a team sport! The whole is greater than the sum of its parts. In this habit, we are to work together for a desired result. However, to do so we have to value the differences in the people we are coming together with.

After I left my home in the wake of many "Lose/Lose" discussions, my wife filed for divorce. I was told she did so out of anger and hurt and really did not want a divorce. However, I called a divorce attorney after receiving the divorce papers in the mail and the attorney promised she would make sure I didn't get "wounded" in the settlement. My wife was led to a divorce attorney that had a reputation for hardnosed settlements, making sure his client "won" the contest.

After nearly a year of alimony and monthly legal fees, I decided to invoke what the 7 *Habits* book calls the "Third Alternative." Because I had been in the Al-Anon program for over forty years, the divorce proceedings were not hostile and I was not angry or upset. I was, however, concerned that we would run out of money before the divorce was finalized. So I called my wife and asked her what she wanted to accomplish in the settlement and maybe we could work out our own solution, so the lawyers did not become rich as we descended more into poverty. Because Ohio is a no-fault state, she was entitled to half the assets of our combined worth. Her answer to my question was to ask for a certain amount of money over the half she deserved. Since I have never been a money person and I would rather pay her the money than the two lawyers, I heartly agreed. The next day, we informed the lawyers and the synergy we created saved us both time and money. Three months after our synergistic Third Alternative, my ex-wife passed away from her disease, but everything was settled and there were no loose ends with her estate.

HABIT SEVEN – SHARPEN THE SAW

This may have been the easiest of the 7 Habits for me. Cutting down a tree is much easier when you have a saw that is sharp. To keep it sharp, you have to take time out to sharpen it periodically to make sure your cutting is both efficient and effective. Taking time out to improve the quality of your life is necessary to get the most benefit from each phase of your life. There is a reason God rested on the seventh day, and it was advised ever since that man take some time off to rest and sharpen the saw.

There are four disciplines that the book suggests we work on to improve our lives. The most obvious is our PHYSICAL health. I have been going to the YMCA for over five decades on a weekly basis. I ride an exercise bike for thirty minutes and then do weight-bearing machines for about twenty minutes at least five times a week. In the summer I bike ride and kayak since I live on a lake. Without being in excellent physical shape, I would not have the energy to teach and travel and take part in other activities that require excellent health. The second is MENTAL health. To sharpen this saw requires reading and writing. This is currently the fourth book I have written, so I enjoy creative writing and I always have one fiction or historical book on my table to read and one book for new knowledge and understanding. Self-improvement is an important daily concept in my life. Covey reads a book a week and limits TV to seven hours during that same timespan. I'm not on his level yet but I am fine with my current practice.

SOCIAL/EMOTIONAL health is the hardest for me because I am a die-hard introvert. I do have a strong family connection with my three local children coming over for Sunday dinner every week, and I see my son in Columbus at least every other month or on holidays. I volunteer at Akron Children's Hospital as a "Roving Reader" every week and am very active in Al-Anon service, as well as helping facilitate a divorce support group at my church. My SPIRITUAL saw is sharpened by attending one Al-Anon meeting every week and church every Sunday. I am in two Bible studies (both on Monday) and pray and meditate daily using the *Calm* app on my cell phone. Some weeks I drive nine hours to my two distant teaching jobs and spend hours listening to Amazon Audible programs, mostly on topics of health and wellbeing. The 7 Habits book recommends at least an hour a day to "Sharpen the Saw" so that you can be at your best in accomplishing all of the six habits that come before the last one or maintenance habit.

Since *The 7 Habits of Highly Effective People* was a book of the eighties, Sean Covey, one of Stephen's nine children, has added a little chapter of his own after each of the 7 Habits. At the end of the book Sean, who has written several complimentary books on his own, summarizes each of the habits in one phrase:

- HABIT ONE – Focus on your Circle of Influence.
- HABIT TWO – Create and live by a personal mission statement.
- HABIT THREE – Focus on your highest priorities.
- HABIT FOUR – Have an Abundance Mentality.
- HABIT FIVE – Practice Empathic Listening.
- HABIT SIX – Seek 3rd Alternatives.
- HABIT SEVEN – Balance production and production capability. (P/PC)

The Al-Anon program has 12 Traditions to go along with its 12 Steps. The traditions help keep the group viable and are the "rules" that keep it functioning as it should. Tradition One states that "Our common welfare should come first; personal progress for the greatest number depends upon UNITY." In the addendum to *The 7 Habits of Highly Effective People*, Stephen Covey states that "UNITY is the biggest fruit of the 7 Habits, and the biggest virtue of the 7 Habits is HUMILITY." If someone asked me to define the Al-Anon program in one word, the word I would use would be HUMILITY. We learn in the program that we do not have all the answers and to get along in the world we need to keep an open mind and be teachable. It also really helps to have a God of your Understanding that is in control. And if they asked me why the Al-Anon program worked in one word, the word given would be UNITY.

COMPASSION
THE FIVE PEOPLE YOU MEET IN HEAVEN
MITCH ALBOM

"The running boy is inside every man, no matter how old he gets."

"All parents damage their children. It cannot be helped."

Heaven is the biggest mystery facing mankind. Does is exist? Where is it? Who gets in and who doesn't? What do you need to do to ascend to this wonderful place, besides "be good and die"?

This is definitely not a religious book, but the concept of an afterlife is one that all religions deal with. The biggest questions are "How do you get in?" and "What is it like when you get there?" Mitch Albom is not a minister or rabbi or religious writer. He is actually a sports writer from Detroit. Since I am a sports fan, I bought his first book, *Tuesdays with Morrie*, and I found nothing about sports but a very heartfelt and emotionally touching interview of an ageing man at the end of his life. It was reporting on the wisdom that Morrie had accumulated over his lifetime, and since I am obviously interested in wisdom the book and author were wonderful discoveries. So I was anxious to find out what Mitch (and Morrie) might have to postulate on the "Kingdom of Heaven."

I have been in three different religions in my life, and they all have very different ideas on the questions I posed above. My father was raised in the religion of his mother (father absent), as so many children are. This religion did not believe in doctors, medicine or surgery, and I really am not sure about their belief in an afterlife. My father was advised to have gallbladder surgery, which he tried to conceal from his church elders, but when they found out they didn't excommunicate him but gave him the cold shoulder and he left the faith. After that, he did not believe in a Higher Power, nor did he believe in Heaven. "When I die, there will just be nothingness—no light, no life, just emptiness. It was like that before I was born, and it will be like that after I die."

My father's fourth or fifth heart attack claimed him at the age of seventy-seven. My fervent hope is that his view of Heaven was wrong. That he is in a place with no heart attacks, no doctors, and no religions. Will I see him after I die? Another good question. Most religions teach that we will see all our relatives and friends, maybe even historical figures that we can talk to and befriend. This is the basis of Mitch Albom's book *The Five People You Meet in Heaven*. In this book, "Eddie" meets five people in the afterlife that have a lesson to teach him. Two are family members, his father and his wife, one is a person he didn't know but who worked where he did, one was his commander in the war in Asia, and one was a child he had never met or known.

Eddie was the handyman at an amusement park called "Ruby Pier." He made sure the roller-coaster and tilt-a-whirl were running and safe. He had done this all his working life and now, at eighty-three, he was still functioning albeit with a bad leg from a war wound. While checking the Demon Drop, a defect causes it to freefall and to save a little girl from death, he pushes her out of the way as the descending ride crushes him to death. I am the same age as Eddie as this is being written, and my hope is that my job of teaching clinical orthodontics does not put me in as much danger of demise as was Eddie.

After Eddie floats around through colorful and panoramic skies, he settles back down to "Heaven" and meets the "Blue Man," who actually worked in the same amusement park where Eddie was killed. He was in the "freak show" because his skin was a blueish color from chemicals he ingested earlier in life. When Eddie asks what killed him, he calmly looked at Eddie and said, "You did!" Turns out when Eddie was a young boy, he chased a baseball into the street while the Blue Man was approaching in his car. He slammed on the brakes and swerved to avoid hitting Eddie and later had a heart attack from the trauma and died. The Blue Man actually thanks Eddie because Heaven is so wonderful and he's glad he made it.

THE LESSON: The first lesson is that there are NO RANDOM ACTS. The ball in the street caused the near accident and subsequent heart attack even though Eddie and his playmates had no idea about the consequences of their simple action. This is close to the idea that "everything happens for a reason," but I don't think it quite embodies that principle. My thought is that some things happen for a reason but there are also coincidences or serendipity or fate that plays out in many instances. The other lesson that resonates more with me is that WE ARE ALL CONNECTED. This reminds me of the "butterfly effect." When the wings of the butterfly move the air around it, the effect goes outward a great distance beyond. When a rock is thrown into a lake, the ripples continue far beyond what the eye can see. In my eyes, this is true. We are all connected and most of us have no idea how far our actions and words carry into the universe.

The second person Eddie meets in Heaven is his Army captain during battle in the Asian Theatre of WWII. Of course, the setting is actually in the combat zone even though they are in Heaven and the depiction is more like the "Hell" of combat. After being captured by the enemy, Eddie and the captain and two others escape and burn down the little town and prison they were being held in. Eddie is slow to leave the scene because he perceives that there is a small figure inside the burning hut and he wants to go back and save this person. Before he can go back inside, he is shot in the leg and has to be helped out of the area to have his wound treated.

Now, in Heaven, his former Army captain informs him that it was actually him that shot Eddie in the leg. He felt he had to do this to get Eddie to give up the idea of rescuing the small figure in the fire and get him out of there to safety. Of course, Eddie is enraged (even in Heaven) because his leg wound and subsequent disfunction has "ruined" the quality of his life.

THE LESSON: The second lesson is that SACRIFICE IS A PART OF LIFE. It's actually something to aspire to. We all must make sacrifices for the greater good of ourselves and the people we serve or represent. There is also a second lesson. This is the lesson of FORGIVENESS. The captain asks Eddie to forgive him for shooting him to get him away from the burning village. "That's what I've been waiting for!" says the captain. Sometimes asking for forgiveness is as hard as granting forgiveness.

After being placed back in uniform in combat environment for the second person and second lesson, Eddie floats through clouds and changing colors and environments until he comes to a small country restaurant. When he peers in the window, he sees the third of the people he is to meet in Heaven. He instantly becomes almost uncontrollably angry when he recognizes a figure in one of the diner's booths—his father. When both Eddie and his dad were living, his father paid little attention to Eddie and when he did pay attention, it was often while abusing Eddie physically and emotionally.

Mitch Albom makes the statement that "all parents damage their children. It cannot be helped." Since I have raised four children, I immediately began to reflect on how this statement replied to me. I know I never laid a hand on any of my children but of course, many parents would say that was how I damaged them. My father "spanked" me with a belt between the ages of seven and eleven, but his lack of attention in my early teen years and then obsessive alcohol consumption affected me more than anything physical. But did his distancing damage me? Did my lack of physical punishment damage my children? Someday I will have to interview my children to see what action or inaction I carried out did them harm.

Mitch writes: "Through it all, despite it all, Eddie privately adored the old man, because sons will adore their fathers through even the worst behavior." I cannot say I adored my father, especially in his drinking years, but I certainly felt a void in my teen life because I had a distant relationship with him. The other quote from this chapter that Mitch forwards is "Parents rarely let go of their children, so children let go of them." Adult children move away, get married, have in-laws, get divorced, change jobs, and have financial and legal problems. One thing I learned from an AA – Al-Anon Couples Group I was in was that no matter how old your children were, their issues and problems were still those of the parents, at least emotionally if not directly.

My situation as a child was different than my situation as an adult. As a teen, I moved out of the house at seventeen to go to school and never really had much relationship with my parents after that. I was home for holidays and a few summers in college but never returned to where they lived, and when they moved to Florida I only visited them once a year. You would think I would have been closer as an only child. Now I have four children and I see the ones who live away from my town at least once a month and the ones who live in town (three) at least once a week!

THE LESSON: The third lesson is very much the same as the second lesson. No matter how much you are maligned and how long you have been wronged, you must FORGIVE. Holding anger is a poison. As we say in the Al-Anon program, "Resentment is like drinking poison and hoping the other person dies." Anger and resentment only hurts those who hold anger and resentment. Eddie's anger wounded him during the years he was alive and now in Heaven, he has to learn to let that go. "Accept, Surrender, Let Go, Let God."

According to Jill Bolte Taylor, M.D., anger is physiologically a 90-second phenomenon. After a minute and a half, you're CHOOSING to remain angry or resenting what happened and the person involved.

Eddie doesn't actually have a dialogue with his father as he did with the first two people he met in Heaven. But he is guided to a life of forgiveness by others from his past who help him to see that even in Heaven, anger is not sustainable and forgiveness is the only path to peace of mind and freedom.

The fourth person Eddie meets in Heaven is his wife, Marguerite. The scene in Heaven is his wedding day and Eddie is deliriously happy, the exact opposite emotion he had when he saw his father. Eddie's wife died many years ago, when they were in their forties. She died after a bout with cancer and Eddie lived the next thirty-six years alone with a feeling of loss and loneliness. Now that they were together again in Heaven, they were "together again."

When you read the obituary page, you often see the deceased with a picture of their previously deceased spouse with the writing above the picture: "Together again." Another of the questions about Heaven would be the presence or absence of committed relationships. The Bible says there are no marriages in Heaven, but do we see former spouses and if so, what is our relationship to them? Since my wife divorced me here on earth, I'm not sure she would even want to see me again in the afterlife.

Even though Mitch Albom promotes the idea of Heaven, there is not much testimony to a God of his understanding. In this chapter, when Eddie and his wife were talking in Heaven, Eddie asked his wife if God knew he was here (in Heaven). Marguerite smiled and said, "Of course!" But Eddie had to admit to her that during some of his life he'd spent hiding from God, and the rest of the time he thought he went unnoticed. Before Al-Anon, this clearly describes my relationship with God!

THE LESSON: The fourth thing Eddie was to learn from the fourth person he met in Heaven was LOVE CONQUERS ALL. Marguerite tells Eddie that life has to end but love doesn't. She felt his love in Heaven even when he was still on earth. That's how strong love can be. Even lost love is still love. When you do things for others out of love, you are getting the first glimpse of Heaven.

The Course in Miracles states that there are only two conditions. They are LOVE and Fear. All that is good comes from the actions and feelings of love, and all that is negative comes from being afraid of something or somebody. Obviously it cannot be verified, but acceptance into Heaven must be based on the amount and quality of the love you have shown during your lifetime. As a Christian, I believe Jesus when he says the only two commandments we need to follow on earth are "Love God with all her heart, soul, and mind" and "Love your follow man as you love yourself." Life is judged more on what you gave than what you have.

The fifth and final person with a lesson to teach Eddie as a newcomer to Heaven is someone he never met or really never saw very clearly. Back in the second lesson, which was during the war, the captain shot him in the leg to get him away from the burning village. The reason he was resisting leaving the dangerous fire is that he thought he saw a small figure in the burning hut, and if it was a person, especially a child, he should go into the fire and rescue him or her. The captain had to shoot him to prevent him from this act that could have cost him his life.

We now find out that there was a little Asian girl in the fire and that was the cause of her death and entrance into Heaven. Of course, when she lets Eddie know that she was the person he saw in the jungle hut fire he collapses in a huge wave of guilt and remorse. He now knows that fire he helped start to burn the enemy village is the fire that killed a five-year-old girl. And then he did not try to save her when he thought he saw a child in the fire.

The little girl asks him to "wash away the scars" she incurred from the burning hut, and he does this as her skin turns back to normal and she finally appears like a normal, healthy little girl. The little girl then tells Eddie what the fifth lesson is.

THE LESSON – Eddie felt that his life was non-essential because he was just a mechanic at an amusement park. The little girl reminded him that he fixed the rides and checked them out before the children rode them. She told Eddie that he kept children safe and that was a great accomplishment and served her as well as all children on earth. Eddie asked the little girl about the little girl he died saving. "Did she live, did I push her out of the way in time?" He said even though he thought he pushed her out of the way, he felt hands pulling him away. The little Asian girl said, "You did keep her safe, the hands you felt pulling you were mine, bringing you to Heaven."

THE LESSON – The last lesson is the most profound, of course. THE THINGS YOU DO FOR OTHERS ARE NOTICED BY BOTH PEOPLE AND GOD. This encompasses some of the other lessons that Eddie learned in Heaven. Obviously, when you Love others you show that love by the things you do for them and the way you treat them. When others offend or oppose you, the forgiveness you give them is noticed by God and by others in your sphere of influence.

In the last "scene" in Heaven, myriads of people of all ages gather on the pier where Eddie's amusement park was located. The author states that they were there because of the simple, mundane things Eddie had done in his life—the accidents he had prevented, the rides he had kept safe, the unnoticed turns he had affected every day in his seemingly lowly function.

As I write this, I am the same age that Eddie was when he was crushed in the Demon Drop accident at an amusement park. Like Eddie, in my 80s I am still working, although my two teaching jobs and one volunteer position at a local hospital are not as life threatening as an amusement park. Even at this seemingly ripe old age, I still have many lessons to learn on Earth before I ascend to learn the lessons in an afterlife. My most fervent daily prayer is to know God's will for me and the power to carry it out while serving others with the talents He has given me.

ACTION
THE FINAL SUMMIT
ANDY ANDREWS

"Adversity is preparation for greatness."

"Direction, not intention, determines destination."

It has been proposed that giving people information, advice, and suggestions works better when it is done in story form. When we are telling our children to be more frugal, we often tell them the story of how we wound up in financial trouble when we first moved out of our parents' house and made poor purchases instead of planning and saving. More is learned by example (story) than just saying "A fool and his money are soon parted" (advice from Proverbs).

The "story" is the gift of Andy Andrews. He has numerous fiction story books, which he uses to get his message of love, forgiveness, trust, hope, and other virtues across to the reader. He also has a love of history and so many of his fiction books take a page out of history and feature characters from ages past, some fictional and some real. As a reader of mostly nonfiction and a lover of self-improvement prose, Andrews' story books give the reader the best of both worlds. The inspirational author also has some nonfiction books, which simply state: "This is how you must act and what you must do!" But it is his story books that make becoming a more ethical and productive person more fun.

My favorite story, and I have read almost all of them, is *The Traveler's Summit*. Some of his stories are about "travelers" or time travelers who go back in time or ahead in time to meet real characters and fictional characters for a teaching purpose. In the first "traveler" story, called *The Traveler's Gift*, a business man named David Ponder has an auto accident and is in a coma. While in this coma, he travels back into history and meets up with other travelers who are all famous and who offer him words of advice or wisdom that he can take back when he "returns" to his conscious state.

One of Andy Andrews' nonfictional books is called *The Seven Decisions*. These are decisions that we all must make if we are to be successful and fulfilled in our lives. But in "The "Traveler's Summit" that we are reviewing, Andrews indicates that each decision comes from a historical character than he met while "traveling."

President Harry Truman gave David Ponder the first decision, which is *THE BUCK STOPS HERE.* The second decision we must make comes from the Bible and King Solomon: *I WILL SEEK WISDOM*. In the first David Ponder Book, *The Traveler's Gift*, he spends time with the Civil War hero Joshua Chamberlin, leading his soldiers from the North. From him comes the third decision: *I AM A PERSON OF ACTION.* The fourth decision is from Christopher Columbus and reads: *I HAVE A DECIDED HEART.* Decision five is from Anne Frank's diary and states: *TODAY I WILL CHOOSE TO BE HAPPY.* As a history buff, Andy must include Abraham Lincoln and the decision he offers is *I WILL GREET EACH DAY WITH A FORGIVING SPIRIT.* The last of the Seven Decisions was given to David Ponder by an angel and not a historical figure. The Archangel Gabriel appears to David and makes him aware of the last decision: *I WILL PERSIST WITHOUT EXCEPTION.*

This sets the stage for this book in which the Archangel Gabriel is really the main character, although not very involved. David Ponder is now an elderly gentleman in his seventies when the Archangel revisits him and invites him to a "Summit." The angel informs David that his Boss (God) is very unhappy with the way things are in the world today and is seriously considering starting over again! David is shocked and can't believe that God would do such a thing until the angel reminds him of Noah and the Great Flood.

The Archangel informs David that there is to be a meeting or summit of all the "travelers" in the history of the world and he is to be the only one still living and the only one not famous either historically or otherwise well known. The meeting purpose is to answer a question that God needs answered correctly in order to save the world. Gabriel then states the rules. The travelers will get five tries to get the answer right, and time will be recorded with an hourglass that has sand draining through it. If none of the five travelers correctly answers the question or if the sand runs through the hourglass and time runs out, God will once again "start over" with a new world.

Then Gabriel hands out the question to be correctly answered: "WHAT DOES HUMANITY NEED TO DO, INDIVIDUALLY AND COLLECTIVELY, TO RESTORE ITSELF TO THE PATHWAY TOWARD SUCCESSFUL CIVILIZATION?" After listing the question, Gabriel appoints David Ponder as the spokesperson for the summit meeting. There are sixty-five other known travelers at the summit, and David can have them all discuss the question and then he can appoint one of them to forward each of the five responses, hoping that one of the famous people can come up with the right answer before time runs out. The one clue Gabriel gives before he leaves is that the answer is basically just TWO WORDS.

I am going to list the "travelers" (deceased) who are at the summit and who are responsible for the solution:

- WINSTON CHURCHILL – most prominent, much of his history elaborated.
- ABRAHAM LINCOLN – second-most prominent, historical background promoted as well, and he provides the second answer or attempt at the solution.

The others are:

- THOMAS (DOUBTING) THE APOSTLE
- DANIEL BOONE
- GEORGE WASHINGTON
- MARTHA WASHINGTON
- SOCRATES
- ARISTOTLE
- FRANKLIN ROOSEVELT
- ELEANOR ROOSEVELT
- LOUIS ARMSTRONG
- FRED ROGERS
- NORMAN V. PEALE
- MARTIN LUTHER KING JR.

- CHRISTOPHER COLUMBUS
- JOAN OF ARC – another major player, historical background and the traveler who comes up with the first guess or answer to the problem
- ALBERT EINSTEIN
- THOMAS EDISON
- BEN FRANKLIN
- GEOFFREY CHAUCER
- MICHELANGELO
- MAHALIA JACKSON
- HELEN KELLER
- CHARLES DICKENS
- REMBRANDT
- ORVILLE WRIGHT
- WILBUR WRIGHT
- DAVY CROCKETT
- MOTHER TERESA
- C. S. LEWIS
- DOUGLAS MACARTHUR
- MARIE ANTOINETTE
- FREDERICK DOUGLASS
- CLEOPATRA
- DR. SCHWEITZER
- EMILY DICKINSON
- MARK TWAIN
- ERIK ERIKSON – major figure, history explained, author of the third solution or answer to the problem proposed by Gabriel
- DWIGHT EISENHOWER
- BERNARD MONTGOMERY
- KING DAVID – major player and author of solution #4
- SOLOMON
- ANNE FRANK – major figure from past "travels" and some history
- GOLDA MEIR
- TEDDY ROOSEVELT
- BEAR BRYANT
- SIR EDMUND HILARY

- PAUL HARVEY
- BOOKER T. WASHINGTON
- GEORGE WASHINGTON CARVER – very major character and the one who proposed the fifth and (supposedly) final solution
- JOHN WOODEN
- JESSE OWENS
- RED GRANGE
- JIM THORPE
- BABE DIDRICKSON ZAHARIAS
- BOB HOPE
- BING CROSBY
- LUCILLE BALL
- NAPOLEON HILL
- OG MANDINO
- NOAH
- MOSES
- HARRY TRUMAN
- WILMA RUDOLPH
- JOSHUA CHAMBERLAIN – the Civil War hero David Ponder met in *The Traveler's Gift*. His history is reviewed, and he is instrumental in the solution, which is actually the sixth and final attempt!

Looking over the long list of summit attendees, it is interesting to see how many of the characters the reader knows. As a senior myself, like David Ponder, I have heard of all of them except Erik Erikson, who was a silent WWII hero. Some of them I have heard of but have little idea of what they did to become famous. It helps that I am a sports fan and a seeker of self-improvement ideas. I know of Joshua Chamberlain and his exploits only because I have previously read *The Traveler's Gift*.

FIRST OF FIVE ATTEMPTS

The first attempt at correctly answering the question is forwarded by Joan of Arc. After discussing her attempts to free France from the British, she says the answer is HOPE. She indicates that hope is the captain of courage and the author of success. Hope sees what is invisible, feels what is intangible, and achieves what most consider impossible. The proof of Hope is that you breathe, and if you are still alive that means you haven't accomplished what you were placed on this earth to do yet.

In the Al-Anon program, HOPE is the Second Step. The first step gets you to admit you are powerless over alcoholism and all else except your own actions. People living with the problem of alcoholism have had to admit that "they are powerless over others and their lives therefore have become unmanageable" (First Step). The Second Step encourages us to "believe in a Power greater than ourselves" (God) that can restore us to proper thinking and acting—and therefore give us HOPE.

David Ponder and the travelers call Gabriel to come back in the room to receive the proposed solution which, in two words, is _RESTORE HOPE._ Gabriel agrees that it is a great solution, but it is NOT the solution he and God are looking for. So back to the meeting room and drawing board for the travelers.

Abraham Lincoln seems to be the traveler most involved in coming up with a second guess at the correct answer. He and a group of travelers believe that the answer may be WISDOM. After all, it is the second of the "Seven Decisions" listed earlier in this and other books. King Solomon is in attendance and the book of Proverbs that he wrote is the wisest writing ever. Winston Churchill notes that "imbeciles and extremists are always so sure of themselves but the wise are those who are full of doubts." Lincoln comments that wisdom is the ability to see, into the future, the consequences of one's choices in the present. Wisdom carries a lot of common sense and Joan of Arc states that she gains a great deal of wisdom by simply remaining silent. One of the travelers came up with what his answer would be when asked to define wisdom—it is the ability to discern. To take the proper path using the available information and prayerfully considering the Will of God.

The two-word answer for this second attempt then is _SEEK WISDOM._ Gabriel is summoned again from behind the summit room door and the answer is forwarded to him. Again, he affirms that this is an excellent choice and validates some of the reasons. However, as he did after the first proposal he firmly stated that this was NOT the answer he and God were looking for and he disappeared from the room in a flash of bright light, leaving the travelers to come up with a third option while the sands of time continued to slither down the narrow neck between the upper and lower glass enclosure.

The discussion about the next answer is where Erik Erikson comes in. In telling about his history during WWII, it was postulated that his actions shortened the war by at least two years! He was able to infiltrate Nazi bureaucracy and pose as a staunch Nazi leader, which led to incredible information to our side that helped turn the tide of the war. Obviously, this was intensely risky because he would be killed if his true identity leaked out and he had to watch soldiers on his side brutally murdered and appear to enjoy it to keep his cover. So of course, because of his war experiences and character, Erik was sure that COURAGE was the ultimate answer. He thought that courage was the resistance to fear and mastery of it, but it is not the absence of fear. The virtue or value of courage appears only when we care very deeply about something or someone. So the two-word answer they wanted to relate to Gabriel was *SHOW COURAGE.*

When they summoned Gabriel and gave him the two-word "guess," he again was pleased with the answer but unmoved. When he told them this was NOT the correct answer or solution, they wanted to ask him questions to help them since they only had two more attempts left and time was not in their favor either. In this question period, Gabriel informed them that this process had happened before to a civilization long before the one we understand. When the travelers asked why this former "world" had ended, he answered, "Arrogance, greed, selfishness, ungratefulness, and loss of faith." But even though this generation is heading in the same path, "it is never too late."

Enter King David to propose a solution or provide answer number four. He goes over his history of infidelity and lust with Bathsheba as well as his slingshot prowess in slaying Goliath. The infidelity was from a lack of self-discipline, but his accuracy with the slingshot was due to the very disciplined practice and prior accomplishments of killing a lion and a bear. So obviously, the good king felt that SELF-DISCIPLINE might be the proper answer. It took self-discipline to practice with his weapon daily, and he states that it really boils down to this question: "Can you make yourself do something you don't particularly want to do in order to get a result you would like to have?" Self-discipline begins with the mastery of your mind. The king states that you should "rule your mind or it will rule you." So the travelers agree to try the two-word solution: *EXHIBIT SELF-DISCIPLINE.*

Gabriel is summoned from behind the summit room door for the fourth time and for the fourth time, the answer is NOT the one he is looking for. He reminds the group of sixty-five or so travelers that they only have one more chance, and the sand seems to be running through the hourglass a little faster now. Time and creative thinking are at a premium.

The fifth traveler to come up with a solution is a humble man who is little known, although his creativity has changed more lives in this country than almost anybody. He is George Washington Carver, and the things he has done with peanuts and other crops to revolutionize the food industry are astounding. David Ponder even muses: "The greatest figures in the history in the world, all together in one room, and it is a former slave that is the most popular person in the place." Carver's solution is simply CHARACTER. Lincoln heartily agrees and states that "Reputation is merely what others think we might be. Character is what we really are. Character is what a man is in the dark." So the whole group heartily endorses the final two-word solution, which is to _BUILD CHARACTER._

When Gabriel is summoned for the fifth and final time and they give him the solution that the group settled on, he seems for the first time to light up and smile, if angels really smile. The celebration begins, thinking that they have found the answer and saved the world.

But hold on a minute! Gabriel stops smiling and shakes his head. This is NOT the right answer and now their five chances have gone, and the demise of the earth as we know it is at hand!

Then Benjamin Franklin interrupted the group and pointed to the hourglass. The sand had not totally run out and he felt that maybe the world could still be saved if time still existed. Some protested that "we only were given five chances and we missed on them all." But Franklin and President Harry Truman believed in the power of PERSISTANCE. In other words, "It's not over till it's over." Accomplishments physically, financially, emotionally, spiritually, and in every other way come to the person or people who persisted without exception.

Just then, the time traveler that David Ponder first met in _The Traveler's Gift_ yelled out from the back of the room, "DO SOMETHING!" And as soon as he shouted that two-word phrase from the audience, the sand stopped running through the hourglass. They quickly summoned Gabriel back in the room and he agreed to give them one more try. So they nervously proposed: *DO SOMETHING.*

Gabriel did not say they were wrong or right, but he smiled and said, "Can you put this in the form of a declaration for me?" And this is what they wrote: "*I cannot do everything, but I can DO SOMETHING. And I can do something right now. Never again will I allow what I cannot do interfere with what I can do!*" The declaration actually fills a whole page, but the "final solution" is one that I totally agree with and after reading this book many years ago, that one bit of advice, wisdom, and direction, has remained with me. In the Al-Anon program, I created my own slogan, which I call my "Nike" slogan: "JUST DO IT AND DETACH FROM THE OUTCOME." Often we fail to DO SOMETHING because we are fearful of the result or lack of result. We may be afraid of embarrassment or failure or even ridicule, but that should never prevent us from doing something when indicated. The second part of my slogan instructs the individual that the outcome is not under our control, so if an action is the right thing to carry out we must do it with little concern whether it turns out the way we want it to or not.

In *The Traveler's Summit*, after discovering that DO SOMETHING is the ultimate world-saving act, Winston Churchill discusses the plight of political parties. "Republicans and Democrats, Conservative and Labor. They have become divided. It is no longer about the country. It is about themselves. And the only cure for humanity is to care again. To come out of their homes and away from their fenced-in lives. It is time to DO SOMETHING."

This book was written years ago but the same situation is even worse today. Congressmen care more about defeating the opposing party and staying in power than DOING SOMETHING beneficial for their constituents and the country at large.

Several years ago, there was a mass shooting in Dayton, Ohio, and nine people were killed. The mayor of Dayton asked the governor to DO SOMETHING to prevent gun violence in our state. Not only did he not do something that would put a stop to senseless killing by guns, but he made it easier to carry concealed weapons, created a "stand your ground" law to allow people to shoot others if they felt threatened and passed a law to allow teachers to have guns in school! Since gun control is a main concern of mine, I DID SOMETHING to bring attention to the problem in our state and country. I have written many letters to local legislators and national senators, governors, and even the president. I have received only a few responses and no forward action, but at least I am DOING SOMETHING!

At the end of the book, the old man David Ponder is interviewed by a reporter about his travels and the knowledge he has acquired by spending so much time with over sixty other famous travelers. The reporter asks David about his interpretation of listening versus hearing. David responds that "The difference in listening closely and actually hearing—UNDERSTAND-ING—there's where the gap exists between great and best! We can know the Truth without having the Best. But we will never have the Best without knowing the Truth."

PROMISE
UNSHAKABLE HOPE
MAX LUCADO

"Build your life on the promises of God. Since his promises are unbreakable, your hope will be unshakable."

"Death, failure, betrayal, sickness, disappointment—they cannot take your hope because they cannot take your Jesus."

My quest to change my life in the mid-seventies was primarily a spiritual outreach fueled by my Al-Anon program. However, I found that although Al-Anon is not a religious program, I could benefit and enhance my spirituality by using religion and going to church and Bible studies, and not just attending one or two Al-Anon meetings a week. The difference between spirituality in the program and religion is that to "work" the program, you need to believe and trust in a "Higher Power" or a "God of your understanding." Religion takes this belief and trust in a more absolute direction in defining that higher power. As a confirmed Christian, my higher power became God, often in the form of his Son, Jesus Christ.

In the late eighties my son, Chris, became involved with a non-denominational Christian group called "Young Life" that was forming at his high school. They met weekly at the houses of each of the students in the group and discussed the Bible and gave personal testimony to how Christ was aiding their journey through high school. After he was in this group for a year, the adult leader asked me if I wanted to be on "the committee." This was a group of adults who met to plan events to raise money for the group, especially to help the kids go to a religious summer camp for a week. We had four adult men on the committee at that time, and the Young Life leader asked us if we would like to start a men's Bible study. The four of us agreed and although the membership of the group has changed many times over the years, we are still going strong thirty-four years later!

Besides reading and discussing the Bible, we often picked out religious books to review, read, and comment on. The author we followed the most, both through books and CDs, was Max Lucado. The San Antonio pastor has authored more books than anyone I know, and his writing still is extremely entertaining and easy to comprehend. The pastor, with a past drinking problem that he is candid about, has a keen wit, a great sense of humor and a deep commitment to teaching Christian principles to both "believers" and those who are slow to this type of faith. He uses many stories (as Jesus did) to teach and create understanding of Bible principles. Some of the stories are personal and some are those he has learned that will prove his points. At the end of each book, there are many pages of questions that can be used for group discussion. I have certainly read at least ten of his books, some for my Bible study and some for my own understanding and faith journey. When I moved out of my house (and marriage) six years ago I left all of my books behind, so when I looked at my current bookshelf I only had two of Max's books to choose from. The one I chose was *Unshakable Hope – Building Our Lives on the Promises of God*. In the foreword, Max proudly states that this is his 40th book, "just like the 40 days Noah floated during the great flood, the 40 years Moses spent in the desert, and the 40 days that Jesus spent in the desert with the Devil." I would guess that Max has written at least ten or twenty more since this one was published.

The reason I chose this writing of the fifty or sixty that Max has published was because the main subject was "Hope." When I came into the Al-Anon program back in 1975, I had no hope. My marriage was shot, my professional life was crumbling, and I was worried, anxious, and emotionally exhausted. No one in my private or professional life told me to hold on to any hope for a brighter future, let alone a brighter present. I used a lot of four-letter words at that time but none of them were HOPE. I liken my situation to being in a large pit in the earth. The pit was ten feet deep and its earthen walls left no place for a foothold to attempt a climb out. There was nothing to grab on to, and although I could look up and see out of the pit all I could envision were gray, overcast skies and no apparent help. Yelling for help was often done in solitude since the few times I tried to "yell" to friends, they told me to keep my troubles to myself.

By some miracle, which I consider the grace of God (my Higher Power), I not only was introduced into the Al-Anon program but I stayed in it out of desperation and survival. The first principle I learned was patience since I wanted salvation and I wanted it now. My Al-Anon teachers gently let me know that serenity or peace of mind was going to take some time to develop and only if I followed the principles of the Al-Anon program, attended weekly meetings, read the literature, and studied under the watchful guise of a sponsor. The second thing I learned was that there was HOPE if I followed the Twelve Steps of AA and Al-Anon. They are basically the same because we are both addicted, the alcoholic to chemicals and the Al-Anon to control. The first step tells us we are powerless and that our lives have become unmanageable. So, where is the hope in that? I knew I had tried everything to get my wife to be a "normal" wife and mother and nothing had worked. "Stay with us," they said. When you get to the second step, the hope starts to seep in. We are told that if we could come to believe in a power greater than ourselves, that power could restore us to sanity. The hope was not in our own devices but in a spiritual power that we could learn to trust and depend upon.

It is this HOPE that Max talks about in his 40th book. The basic premise in this writing is that we are to have hope because of the promises of God in the scriptures. I am not sure who counted them, but Max indicates that God has made 7,487 promises in the Holy Bible that he cannot break. Every one of them is offered to build up the confidence and hope of all mankind, who were "made in his image."

Because this is a religious Christian writing, the devil is featured as a "divider," or an entity that will strip hope from you if you stray from belief and trust in God. Divisions such as divorce and resentments come from the devil as well as temptations. But Max indicates that if you are a believing person, "God will not let you be tempted any more than you can tolerate." The weapons we have in religion against evil and the devil are prayer, worship, and scripture.

Part of the hope we have of a bright present and future comes from the "grace" of God or his favor, which we did not earn nor deserve. But Max indicates that this grace may not extend to the people with false pride. He states that "God resists the proud but gives grace to the humble." Religion and the

Al-Anon program both rely on the humility of the believer. We cannot do it alone. Someone or something higher than us can help us out of the pit in the earth and instill a brighter future.

Max emphasizes that prayer impacts the actions of God. This gives us the hope that if we pray and talk to God on a continual basis, he will hear our needs and wants and possibly act in our favor. And if he doesn't give us what we want, it may be an indication that what we want is not really that good for us and he has something better in mind. I used to tell my Sunday School teens that if you want to stay out an hour later on Friday night, it won't happen unless you ASK your parent. They may say no but they may say yes, so always ASK. As Wayne Gretzky often quoted, "You miss 100% of the shots you don't take."

The Christian hope of salvation or our existence after our death in this world is based on faith in Jesus Christ. It has nothing to do with how much you accomplished, how much you helped others, how important you become, how you uplifted humanity. It is only based on the belief that Jesus in the Son of God and was resurrected from the dead three days after his crucifixion. Because of his life after death, it is believed that all believers will be resurrected into the next "world." This indeed is a great reason for hope no matter what kind of life we are leading presently on this planet.

While we are on this plane, we can have hope for love, joy, peace, forbearance, kindness, and faithfulness because these positive traits are the fruits we receive from the Holy Spirit or the third part of the Trinity of God. So for Christians who have faith, there is hope for good things in this life and even better things in the next.

Although I am a confirmed Christian, I have trouble with some of the principles espoused by Max and other ministers in that only "believers" are accepted into the realm of "Heaven" and those who do not profess to believe in Christ are doomed to Hell or someplace less than Heaven. I have not had a lot of Jewish friends, but the ones I know are better citizens and promoters of kindness, graciousness, and love than many committed Christians. I am almost sure my friend and colleague Harvey has received the same just desserts in death as have the good Christians I know.

As I used to tell my religious education students in the Catholic Church, "You don't have to believe everything the Church does in order to be Catholic." After all, the Church did away with "limbo" (Purgatory for kids) when my second son was baptized. Before I was confirmed, I took Holy Communion (which tasted like bread and wine to me) and if I ever get married again (I won't), I won't bother with an "annulment." Now that I am in a Methodist denomination, the Church is splitting from the United Church because they oppose gay marriage and gay clergy, which doesn't sit well with me. Hope for me is that the love that Christ portrayed, demonstrated, and taught 2000 years ago will prevail and my faith journey will exemplify that love through my thoughts, actions, words, and deeds.

COMPANIONSHIP
THE FIVE LOVE LANGUAGES: The Secret to Love that Lasts GARY CHAPMAN

"Psychologists have concluded that the need to feel loved is a primary human emotional need."

"I had discovered in the earlier years of my own marriage the difference between the 'in-love' experience and the 'emotional need' to feel loved. Most in our society have not yet learned that difference."

Stephen Covey spoke often in his 7 *Habits* book about the "emotional bank account." This referred to the idea that we are all either adding to or subtracting from the "bank accounts" of every person we encounter. Being kind adds to the account and being oppositional subtracts from it. In *The Five Love Languages* Gary Chapman discusses the same concept, although he calls it the "love-tank." Since he is a marriage counselor and psychologist, his paradigm is the relationship between married couples. As he has counseled hundreds of couples over the years, he has noticed that divorces occur when the "love-tank" is on empty and he gives his clients ideas on how to fill the spouse's love-tank to make the marriage functional (and loving) again.

The misconception of most people is that the "in-love" experience must be sustained during the whole course of the marriage or relationship. Chapman teaches that romantic obsession lasts only two years from the beginning of the relationship or even less. After that, the couple makes the CHOICE to stay together and works daily on uplifting and supporting their spouse. The relationship becomes "What can I do for you today?" rather than "What can you do for me?"

My wife and I went to a Catholic "Marriage Encounter" about one year after she came out of treatment for chemical dependency. It may have been the highlight of our forty-eight-year marriage, as she was newly sober and in AA and I was firmly ensconced in the Al-Anon program. We still walked around with a "program glow" and thought a weekend retreat to enhance the new relationship was a great idea. It was there that the priest running the weekend told us that "Love is a DECISION, not a feeling." Love is a verb and not a noun. Of course, romantic love is necessary to bring the couple together but "true" love, which requires work and effort, is necessary to allow them to stay together for the long term.

Since Chapman was convinced that filling your spouse's "love-tank" was essential to a fulfilling marriage, he became interested in what marriage partners wanted most from their spouses to fill that tank. His discovery was that not all people respond favorably to the same type of "loving" behavior. In this book, he postulated that there were basically five "love languages" that differentiated people in how they would like to be loved. The five are "Words of Affirmation," "Quality Time," "Gifts," "Act of Service," and "Physical Touch." We all respond to one of these languages more than any of the other four, although we may be high in two and some may claim to want all five.

During the good years of my marriage, Sally and I were in a "Couples Club," which was made up of seven married couples that were either in AA or Al-Anon. We had to be active in one of these programs for at least a year and married for at least a year. I truly think that our marriage would have ended far sooner had we not participated in this monthly "club." We would meet at the house of one of the couples and discuss a topic chosen by the host. Because Sally and I did not share a lot on an intimate level, these meetings forced us to dialogue about our relationship and spiritual growth at least one day a month. A couple with both spouses in an active recovery program is a wonderful way to a happy, functional relationship, and the couple's club just enhanced it that much more.

Of course, some of our couples sessions revolved around discussing Gary Chapman's concept of *The Five Love Languages*. This is where we discovered the love languages of our spouse and then made attempts to match the results and improve our marriage. My wife was a reader of fiction even though she was a psychologist and I'm sure she never read Chapman's book, so the group dynamic was good for those who had not stumbled upon this classic piece of information.

WORDS OF AFFIRMATION

Since this is definitely my strongest language of love, I will start with this one. For most of my life, I have always wanted to be praised and given complimentary words. Was it because my father never praised me much or because I was an "approval addict" or a perfectionist, I can't say. My degree was in dentistry, not psychology. However, I always longed to be validated, either directly or in writing. All my life I have sent cards and thank-you notes to people. I always buy cards with no writing on the left page so I can write a whole section myself to uplift the recipient. As Chapman reminds us, if our primary love language is words of affirmation we will tend to use that language to relate to others even when it may not be their primary language.

It always bothered me when I received a birthday or Valentine's card from my wife with just two written words on it: "Love, Sally"! I needed more than two words! Of course, the card would be full of wonderful words on all sides of the card, but they were printed from the manufacturer and not from the pen and the heart of the one who was supposed to love me. Because my wife's "love language" was not "words of affirmation," it never occurred to her that my love-tank was not being filled no matter how expensive or wordy the cards were.

Chapman's writing points out that compliments, encouraging words, and kindness fall under this first love language. Also, making amends and granting forgiveness is a feature of this form of language. When one makes requests instead of demands of the other person, they are enhancing the relationship. On the other hand, criticism, harsh words, sarcasm, putting the other down verbally or with body language is a huge love-tank drainer. Even the silent treatment severely wounds a person who values "words" as their love language. The book offers a quote from an unknown source: "The tongue has the power of life and death."

QUALITY TIME

This "love language" is chiefly spending time with the other person. In this generation, many couples sit with each other but look at their phones. If one of them has quality time as their love-tank filler, this will not work. The key word is QUALITY. We must give the other our undivided attention. The most important things to fill the tank of these people is to (1) ASK QUESTIONS, and (2) LISTEN. It is very much in alignment with the sixth habit in the *7 Habits* book: "Seek to understand before you seek to be understood."

Gary Chapman states that a couple that has one person demonstrating this love language should have a daily habit of talking about three things that happened to them that day and how they felt about it.

Because this language was not high on my wife's or my list, we didn't demonstrate it and were not terribly affected because of the lack of it. I truly think our marriage would have been enhanced by more quality time, but our love-tanks were kept half full rather than emptied because of our daily habits. When I came home, I said hello and then retired to my den to read the paper or read something until the call for dinner. When my wife came home from a meeting or work, she never came into my den and sat down to tell me things or even ask me things. Both of us would have been shocked if that had happened. We had a huge house (each of us had our own den), and we could be in the house for hours with each other before we were together and had any dialogue.

GIFTS

This was my spouse's primary love language. Unlike me, she loved clothes, shoes, fancy appliances in the home and she loved to shop. Maybe the best thing I did to show her love was to go shopping with her and let her take as long as she wanted in each shop without insisting that she hurry up or we move on to lunch or home. Many times I would stand or sit outside the shop while she perused and made up her mind about what and how much to purchase. I usually validated her purchasing whims, and my gift was usually paying for it.

"Gifts" is at the bottom of the totem pole on my love-language scale. So it was hard at first to realize how important receiving gifts was to my wife and my children with that love language. I really do not like "stuff." When someone gives me a gift, I have to decide how to use it, where to put it, and now I have to write words of affirmation for something I didn't want. In my retirement life, I only own one thing of value: a 2018 Subaru. I do not own the house I live in, I sold my office building, my practice, my large home, my condo in Florida, and the less I have the better I like it. When people buy me gifts, it gives me just one more unwanted item to take care of and account for. My daughter has purchased snowblowers and power washers for my house. I continue to shovel and hire professional power washers as needed.

The importance of gifts to my wife may have ended my marriage, or at least added to its demise. In 2016 our marriage was hanging by a thread, but we still were close enough to live together and celebrate the Christmas season. My wife has always loved bathroom scales. She has always had one and used it, although I never cared to know about my weight. While shopping for gifts for her, I found a scale at Bed Bath & Beyond that not only gave your weight but BMI, blood pressure, and other features. I thought she would be thrilled! When I told friends that I purchased a scale for my wife, they all commented, "What were you thinking? You never buy a woman a scale." Because of that "gift" and other things she refused to go to Florida with me in January, and in February I told her I was moving out.

ACTS OF SERVICE

"Actions speak louder than words." Well, not in my case but for many, doing things for your spouse or loved one is what fills their emotional love-tank. Of course, you have to do these things for your significant other with a "positive spirit." If you do chores or helpful deeds begrudgingly, it will not count and the tank will drain. In modern times, the household roles have undergone a dramatic change. In my parents' day, the household chores such as cooking, cleaning, laundry, and child raising were done by the woman. The man paid the bills, took care of the car, was the primary breadwinner, and fixed anything that was broken. Today, those roles are not as well defined, so you need to determine each spouse's normal duties and then serve them by doing it or helping them do it cheerfully. If you know that acts of service is your spouse's love language, you should ask them to make a list of ten things he or she would like for you to do during the next month.

When our couples club discussed the love languages and my wife's was clearly gifts, she felt somewhat greedy, as if gifts was not a very desirable love language. She immediately decided that her "new" or "chosen" gift was acts of service. This made her feel better emotionally even though it was not really true. However, gifts of service was high on the list of things that filled her tank, and I often made an attempt, although feeble, to accommodate this desire. I can't cook but always brought home carryout when I knew she was busy or needed a break. I'm not good at house cleaning but paid people to come in and do the work on a biweekly basis. I was in a men's retreat when I heard another man say he made coffee for his wife every morning before she got up. At that time, I didn't drink coffee, but I thought this would be a fairly easy act of service so I did this for many years during our marriage. I truly think Sally appreciated this act but never gave me words of affirmation for my efforts.

My oldest daughter is very much like my wife in that gifts and acts of service are high on her short list of love-tank fillers. She not only brings me gifts almost weekly such as new silverware, grocery items, and cleaning supplies, but she cleans my garage, shovels my driveway, and rearranges my cabinets and even takes my trash back to her dumpster rather than put it in my trash bin. I have lived in my house for over five years and so far I have never purchased any toilet paper! If acts of service and gifts were my tank fillers, I would be overflowing with love and gratitude. However, I continue to remind her to "Please ask me if I want a gift or something done before you carry out the act." I think this question can prevent a gift giver and service provider from overstepping their bounds and draining a person's tank.

TOUCH

Growing up in a family with a distant father and no siblings or close relatives probably set me up to live without touch as a major factor. My mother was all about touch but for some reason, I would fend her off whenever she tried to hug or kiss me. The first time I ever hugged my father or told him I loved him was after he was retired and living in Florida. I had been in Al-Anon for a few years and in that program, we hug everyone in sight before and after the meeting. When I first hugged him he wasn't shocked and I think he was glad I made the effort, although no words were forthcoming to indicate that fact.

This last of the five love languages is my "secret second." It had been lying dormant in my psyche and habits for many years until the warmth and touch of the members of Al-Anon brought it out. Although my wife was in the AA program, touch and hugging were not her favorite forms of communication. She used sort of a "half-hug" with one arm around the other's shoulder while she faced sideways rather than toward the person she was hugging. She was always very much concerned with "personal space" and recoiled when asked to sit too close to other people.

When we went to our marriage encounter after sobriety, we were taught that we should hold hands as often as possible. For years we held hands while driving in the car until the console and cup holders made it difficult. We held hands during mass in the church and continued to do that until she quit going to church a few years before we divorced. I'm not sure either one of us felt comfortable with handholding because we were both aware that the other person probably did not want to do that.

At a dental lecture I went to early in my career, the speaker said that we should "always touch your patient before they leave the office as a gesture of love and closeness." As an orthodontist, we have much shorter appointments than other dentists, so we need something to show the patient we care and touch was advised as the ideal gesture. So I always touched my patient on the left shoulder (I am left-handed) before I got up from the chair and they were dismissed. Even in this day of fear of human contact, I truly think that one act bonded me with my patients and enhanced our relationship.

Gary Chapman is a psychologist who specializes in marriage counseling. He is amazed at the number of couples who come in complaining that "He says he just doesn't love me anymore." Or revealing to him that "We don't connect, and our love has grown cold." The counselor then informs the couple that love is not a connection, it is a CHOICE. You are in the marriage to bring love to the other person, not yourself. The choice to love has to be made every day for a committed married couple.

Chapman feels that whether you know your spouse's love language or not, you can help your relationship grow by playing the "Tank Check Game" three times each week. At those sessions, you are to ask your spouse for a reading of 0 to 10 regarding the fullness of their love-tank. Then if the reading is low, ask for suggestions of your spouse to raise that number for the next check. If your spouse is at a 10 consistently, you can pat yourself on the back—but don't stop loving!

Gary Chapman speaks little about religion or spirituality in his book, but in the last chapter he admits he is a committed Christian. He is strongly influenced by the gospel of Luke and he quotes a few passages from that gospel, including loving the unlovable or difficult. He emphasizes Jesus' teaching that we are to not only love those who are easy and comfortable to love but we need to make a choice to "Love your enemies, do good to those who hate you, bless those who curse you, pray for those who mistreat you." Like almost all the sages, we find wisdom in the spirituality of the sage and author.

BLESSED

THE BLESSING
GARY SMALLEY AND JOHN TRENT

"The Lord bless you and keep you; The Lord make His face to shine upon you, and be gracious to you; The Lord lift up his countenance upon you, and give you peace."

"The act of touch is a key to communicating warmth, personal acceptance, affirmation—even physical health!"

When you raise two different generations of children, you raise them quite differently. That may seem surprising, but a twenty-year difference brings a huge change in parenting practices as well as culture change and also a big difference in the age of the parents. Our birth children were born in 1969 and 1971 and were a part of Generation X.

Twenty years later we decided we wanted two more children, so we adopted a daughter in 1988 and a son (from El Salvador) in 1991. If you want four children, this is not a bad way to raise them since you only have half of the expense and half of the trials and tribulations even though you are actively parenting for forty years!

With our first set, we had family meetings and "spiritual time" weekly. The spiritual time was a half-hour meeting where we would read and discuss some spiritual or religious material that I would find and provide. Twenty years later, we still had family meetings but had difficulty establishing a "spiritual time," for some reason. We did read to the second set of kids and say prayers with them at bedtime but no formalized session of reading spiritual or religious material.

However, I came upon the idea of "blessing" each of my adopted children every night before they went to bed or before I left the house knowing I would not be back before bedtime. As with many of the lessons learned from the "sages," I am not totally sure where I heard Smalley and Trent's idea of blessing my kids at bedtime. I am sure that I did not read their book, *The Blessing*, because after reading it I realized I was not giving the blessing as I should have or as least not encompassing the five features of the blessing that the authors emphasize. Much of the teaching of the "sages" came from CDs or audiotapes or just articles written by them about their major philosophy and principle.

My concept of the blessing was to place my hand on their forehead and then recite the Biblical blessing from the book of Numbers 6:24-26, which was the words of Aaron, the brother of Moses: "The Lord bless and keep you; The Lord make His face to shine upon you, and be gracious to you; The Lord lift up His countenance upon you and give you peace." I'm not even sure that I got all the words to this blessing in the right order, but the idea was there. I was giving a father's blessing to his young children each night along with the quality of touch, which is so important to children as well as adults. When reciting the passage from Numbers, I always wondered what "countenance" meant since I was wishing that upon my children every night. Wikipedia indicates that it relates to "the beatific vision of the face of God." My two Generation Y children got so used to the "blessing" that they would seek me out before going to bed to make sure they received the daily recitation. Sometimes when I was out for the evening, they would accost me in the morning and challenge me with "You forgot to give me the blessing last night!" It became very important for them to receive that, which was rightfully theirs every single evening.

Before I read Smalley and Trent's book, I was not aware of how religious they are. Both are firm Christians and much of the book focuses on evangelism for the Christian faith. There are many references to the Bible and actions and words of Christ to explain life as it should be. I too am a Christian but am not one that looks to Christian authors for my personal-improvement quest, although five of the thirty sages I will feature are strong Christians.

The authors start by giving the Old Testament origination of the blessing. Isaac was tricked into blessing his younger son, Jacob. In those days only the older Hebrew son could receive the blessing, and for years Esau pursued Jacob to kill him because he took the blessing that rightfully belonged to the older son. Then when he finally forgave Jacob and they reconciled, Jacob married and had many sons and "blessed" his second-youngest son, Joseph. The other brothers were miffed because he "stole" their blessing, and their angst prompted them to sell him to slave traders in Egypt. In those days, the blessing had a lot more significance and consequence than today.

What I failed to learn when I started giving my young children the blessing was that there are five elements to each blessing. You not only must TOUCH the person you are blessing and say positive blessing WORDS, but you must bless them with words of HIGH VALUE and a PROSPEROUS FUTURE, with a sense of total COMMITMENT.

So obviously the blessing from Numbers in the time of Moses is not enough! My words were always the same to both children and did not praise, predict a bright future, nor show my unswerving commitment. I needed to say more and change the blessing not only day to day but offer a different blessing to each child.

TOUCH was the one thing I got right. Although it was just a hand to the forehead, it was better than a handshake. I really did not learn to hug until I got into the Al-Anon program, and even there it was years before I was comfortable hugging others, especially men. As I wrote previously, my father never really had a father since his left home when he was an infant and only reappeared when he needed cash for alcohol. So he never hugged me or said much to me affectionately at all. I was close to forty in the Al-Anon program when I first hugged my father and told him I loved him. When you grow up as an only child and your father does not touch you (except for punishment), this becomes difficult to overcome as an adult and loving parent. Trent and Smalley indicate that you truly need ten touches a day to maintain a healthy presence. I always had a dog and hugging that dog probably got me through my teen years and beyond. Somewhere in my professional reading, an author of a dental magazine said that he touches every one of his patients on the shoulder before dismissing them from his chair. I began doing that early in my career and even though it was uncomfortable at first, I can't believe the positive relationships I developed with my patients.

WORDS of affirmation is my primary love language, although I now believe that touch is a high second. One of the Ten Commandments is "Thou shall not kill." This does not just refer to murder. Harsh words can kill someone's spirit or kill their ambition and desires.

In our Al-Anon program, our outreach is to "Encourage and understand the alcoholic." Encouraging is the use of positive, uplifting words, whereas criticism and negative feedback can wound severely. One of my daughters was having trouble in school with basic courses and we had reason to believe she might not even pass. At dinner one night, she told her mother and me that she might want to become a doctor someday. My wife laughed and stated, "With your performance in school, you have as much chance of becoming a doctor as a snowball in Hell." Those words were crushing, not encouraging, and my daughter had a lot of trouble overcoming that "reverse blessing" bestowed upon her. Today she is a nurse and is very bright and successful in business and life and is a foster parent. Many children who get negative words and no blessing overachieve to get noticed and become very discouraged when that doesn't work. As a perfectionist, I have trouble praising others because they are supposed to perform ideally so when they do, why praise or thank them for it? As a teacher now, I am learning how to praise the student and the patient they are working on even though it doesn't come naturally.

The next two features of the ideal blessing are personalized to the person you are blessing. HIGH VALUE is indicated when you do not limit your praise to a result they achieved. Blessings are not earned but tell the person how much they are valued for just who they are. Using a "word picture" works well here. Like "You are my rock of Gibraltar" or "You are Superman and Batman rolled into one." The SPECIAL FEATURE part of the blessing is when you tell them about a certain quality that makes them who they are, such as "You have a very sensitive and warm heart" or "You have wisdom far beyond your age."

The COMMITMENT feature of the blessing is to just show the person you are blessing that you "say what you mean and mean what you say." The biggest part of this commitment, as it is with any communication, is LISTENING. This is where you show your interest, provide encouragement, and even admonish if that will be helpful and positive. Be honest, show integrity so your blessing can be believed.

After explaining the features of a good blessing, Gary Smalley and John Trent discuss giving the blessing to each other as married couples. Then they move on and talk about blessing friends, working colleagues, and even parents. Unfortunately, I am retired (mostly) and am not married and my parents are long gone. So I can still bless my four children, one grandchild and numerous friends in the Al-Anon program. Everyone in the program is encouraged to get a sponsor and they are the ones that we can have tough, intimate discussions with and the ones that are most likely to bless us. The family of Al-Anon is far more functional that most people's family of origin.

Smalley and Trent even tell readers where to go if family and friends are not blessing them as they should. As Christians they mention Young Life, a non-denominational program for teens that two of my children benefitted from. The Big Brother/Big Sister program is wonderful for kids who have one or more parents gone or nonfunctional. I have benefitted from this program by having two "little" brothers over the years. The first had a missing father and the second had no parents and grew up with an angry grandmother. I can guarantee that the second one received no blessing at all in his situation and the first may have had some affirmation from his mom and stepdad. I still see both of them, although one is fifty years old, married and doing well, and the second is twenty-two years old, single and still struggling to mature properly.

My prayer is that my daughter, whom I blessed when she was a preteen, will bless her young son, who is approaching the one-year mark. It's hard to believe that I have four children over the age of thirty and only one grandchild to show for it. It is never too late in life to both bless those people around you but also be a blessing to them by demonstrating how to serve and love.

DIRECTION
9 THINGS YOU SIMPLY MUST DO
DR. HENRY CLOUD

"Those who succeed in life cannot ignore their hearts, minds, and souls."

"Déjà vu people do not make decisions based on fear or other people's reactions."

My wife was trained as a nurse but after recovering from chronic alcoholism, she decided to shift careers and become a psychologist so she could counsel addicts. She received a B.A. from Malone College and a Master's in Psychology at Walsh College and then set up her own practice in our little Northeast Ohio town. About that time, my spiritual journey was seeking practical living solutions from not only motivational and religious leaders but due to my wife's influence, I looked to modern psychology to provide me with ideas for personal as well as spiritual growth.

My Al-Anon program teaches us how to set proper boundaries with those in our lives and I had read Dr. Cloud's book on *Boundaries* (he was a coauthor) before coming upon a book stating that there were just simply "9 things" you must do. What an intriguing title! A psychologist was going to reveal the nine things you simply must do—for what? Was it to gain enlightenment, to be happy, to be successful, to be closer to God, to earn the love and respect of colleagues and friends? It was hard to pass up a book with such a demanding and, at the same time, encouraging title.

Like many of the other authors I have reviewed and will review, Henry Cloud uses Biblical quotes and concepts from both testaments of the Bible to back up his claims and support his theories. At this time in my spiritual journey,

I was becoming more "religious" because I believe it helped my spiritual quest and because I was teaching religious education (Sunday School) to eighth-graders at St. Paul's Catholic Church of North Canton.

The second quote of the two that I used in the introduction to this book and author refers to "Déjà vu" people. In the prologue to the *9 Things*, Dr. Cloud discusses similar characteristics and qualities that all successful people have. When he was in the presence of one of these people, he felt like he had "met this person before" and he knew that they would be a success and respected by people no matter where they were from or where they were going. The nine qualities he outlines in this book are present in all of the outstanding people he has interacted with, and it becomes very apparent when he is in the presence of one of them because the same outstanding characteristics keep repeating over and over in the same way in each one of them.

THE NINE THINGS:

"DIG IT UP."

All of us have desires and talents inside that we are born with or have developed over time. Dr. Cloud feels that the two most powerful forces that people carry are TALENT and DESIRE. It is what we do with that talent and desire that makes the optimum impact for the individual and for the world in general. The Bible verse of the "Talents" is used as an example. In this parable of Jesus, a man gives three people under him some "talents" to take care of for him while he is away. Two of the three use the talent to make twice what they were given, whereas the third just buries the talent so that nothing is lost. Because of their stewardship, the two who made the most are given more and the one who made nothing is turned away in disgust. Déjà vu people are those who take risks. Pain or conflict do not stop them. They always take action! The first of the nine things is to "dig up" whatever you have within (talent, money, skills, leadership) and use it for the benefit of those you care about and serve.

"PULL THE TOOTH."

As a dentist, I slightly object to Dr. Cloud using a dental reference as an example of the second of the nine "things you must do." How about a root canal instead of an extraction? However, what he is trying to convey is that if there is something negative in your life, get rid of it. As far as "things" go, this is not a problem for me. I actually love to purge unnecessary items from my house and life. Separating from negative people, however, has been much harder for me. I worked for fourteen years with a business partner that didn't help build the business and actually caused a decline, and it was my new partner that finally talked me into pulling the plug (or extracting the tooth). People who hate their jobs but keep working there out of habit or lack of initiative to find something they do like has never made sense to me. Life is too short for unsatisfactory living experiences. The Serenity Prayer tells us to "change the things we can" and that includes purging what is bringing us down.

"PLAY THE MOVIE."

Almost all of our sages talk about the value of GOALS. It is in this third of Dr. Cloud's "nine things" where goals are first discussed. The "movie" he discusses is to imagine the outcome in the future after the action you are taking or not taking today. How does the movie end when you seek a certain outcome or goal that may not be good for you or others? If you continue in this dysfunctional relationship, how will your life turn out? If you always wanted to be an orthodontist but are forty years old, the movie shows that at age fifty you could be a successful orthodontist with a great practice if you just have the fortitude to take the plunge. You could even practice for thirty years at age fifty! I practiced until age seventy-seven and then have helped out and taught in my eighties. Using the "movie" of the future will help you make decisions that will change your life for the better. And when you have the goals to do that, you have to have an action plan to reach those goals.

"DO SOMETHING."

This may be my favorite of the "9 things." Sometime ago in Al-Anon, I came up with my own slogan: "Just do it and detach from the outcome." I call this my Nike slogan. I am a big advocate in taking action. Another Al-Anon concept is the "Three A's"—Awareness, Acceptance, and Action. You must be aware of a situation, accept that it has happened, and then act to make it better or resolve the issue. Stephen Covey, in his 7 *Habits*, mentions one as being "proactive" or taking action. We have already discussed Andy Andrews' book, which promotes the concept of "doing something." Although I advocate prompt action, I must admit that I am slow to apologize, slow to make amends, slow to confront others even for their benefit. I have been on a dating service for a few years, and I often surmise that a person will not like me because I am too small or too old, so I don't send them a message. Fear of failure and rejection are stumbling blocks to an active mindset. Being an "approval addict" also makes the personal risk higher. As a spiritual seeker, I do pray for God to help me with an action, but the Bible tells us that He "only helps those who help themselves." We have to do our part and take the action required.

"ACT LIKE AN ANT."

For this Déjà vu characteristic, it would help to buy an ant farm. Then you could watch each ant carry one grain of sand at a time and over a few weeks, an entire village would be born. How did that happen—one grain of sand at a time. In the Al-Anon program, the slogan is "One day at a time." That is even the title of our longstanding daily reader. For the alcoholic, if they can just make it through the day without drinking they are a success. Just focus on one thing at a time, one day at a time. Live in the present and don't be overwhelmed or worried by future endeavors or tasks. Sometimes, as I read the books I've committed to for this book, I become anxious and want to "skim" to get through them faster. But I know that if I do that I might miss something really good that will improve the quality and impact of this book, so I resist the temptation. On my bathroom mirror is a paper with my "four P's for success." The first two are Patience and Perseverance. To act like an ant, you have to have these qualities in large amounts to practice the Al-Anon slogan "Easy does it—but do it!" By the way, the other two "P's" are Positivity and Posture.

"HATE WELL."

The word hate never resonated well with me, so this is my second-least favorite "thing you must do," after pulling teeth. Dr. Cloud's premise here is that there are things we should hate. The Bible in Proverbs talks about the seven things that God hates. So if God can hate, we should be able to as well. When I tried to think of things I hate, I came up with a few. I hate surprises. I hate evil. As I write this, it is -5 degrees with a 40-mph wind, and I hate going out in this weather. As I thought more about what is currently going on in the world and our country, I realized that I hate war, I hate political division, and I hate guns. Dr. Cloud points out that hating injustice or "things" is good and necessary, but we should not hate individuals. He points out that we should not tolerate things we hate but act to resolve them as Déjà vu people would. I have written letters to politicians about gun control to little avail, but the effort made me feel better. Déjà vu people would act to resolve conflict and not let it fester. My kids always used the "hate" word and I actually hated to hear it. There were kids at school they hated, and they hated school and church and bedtime and even dinners cooked by Dad. Now adults, my four kids do not use the word "hate" much around me anymore but there are things they should hate, and my hope is that they will "do something" about those things.

"DON'T PLAY FAIR."

This doesn't sound like a worthy objective. Don't we teach our kids to "play fair" when they go outside to join their friends? However, the quality person or Déjà vu person always plans to give more than they get. As Jesus said in the Sermon on the Mount: "We should be more concerned with giving instead of getting. No more tit for tat" (*The Message*). After all, the concept of Grace in the Bible is that we are getting better than we deserve. This is not equal or even fair. We are to be giving without thinking of a reward. When asked by a couple we were "counseling" in our church before marriage, I said the most important thing to remember if you want your marriage to last is that the relationship will never be 50-50. One of the partners will always be giving more than the other. Just not always the same one. Speaking of divorce, when I was unfortunate enough to be going through one, the fair thing would be to divide our assets down the middle. But the attorneys were looking for more for their side. Finally, in desperation, I called my wife and said, "What will it take to get this settled without the attorneys involved?" She wanted more than half the money involved. This was not fair, but I gladly gave her what she wanted and, in doing so, felt better about myself and saved more than the amount I acquiesced to her in attorney fees. The act of forgiving is also acknowledging that what happened was not fair but it doesn't help anyone to hold on to anger or hate.

"BE HUMBLE."

If someone ever asked me to sum up the Al-Anon program in one word, that word would be HUMBLE. When faced with living with an alcoholic, I thought I had to solve the issues and I was the only one who could get my wife to act like a "normal wife and mother." The program teaches us that we don't have all the answers. That there is a power greater than ourselves that is in control. That other people with more experience and strength could direct us to a more serene way of life. A humble person admits he needs help. Humble people are teachable. At least I was humble enough to stay in the program for many years and learn what true humility entailed. Oprah Winfrey stated that "Humility is not thinking less of yourself, it's thinking of yourself less." It takes true humility to admit mistakes and accept failure with no excuses. Humble people receive correction as well as confrontation gracefully. They are grateful for others' help and they seek to understand others rather than seeking to be understood. They are always interested in what is best for the other and carry no defensiveness. We recently had a president who was the opposite of humble. Not only did he insist that HE was the only one who could solve the world's problems, but he was so defensive that he could never let a negative comment about him go without responding in an indignant manner. Humility isn't taught, it is born with experience and character. And it is present in all Déjà vu people.

"UPSET THE RIGHT PEOPLE."

The last of the "9 things" is one of the hardest for me. As the consummate "people pleaser," I do not like to upset anyone. This is a part of my "disease," which brought me to Al-Anon and has me still working on being able to say what I have to say and act when action is not popular with all concerned. In the Al-Anon program, we have several sayings that speak to this mandate. One is "Say what you mean; mean what you say; just don't say it mean." Communication issues may have caused my divorce or at least made my marriage less than ideal. I never wanted to upset my wife, so I would withhold issues that needed to be discussed out of fear of conflict or a lose-lose discussion. I had one staff person in my employ that was a loser from week one, yet I waited a long time before I confronted her and an even longer time before I fired her. After twenty-one years with my first business partner, I was going to leave the practice until my Bible study fellows asked me if I had discussed my issues with him. Of course, I had not because I didn't want to upset him. The subsequent talk went well, and we practiced together for another eighteen years. Another Al-Anon slogan is "NO is a complete sentence." A Déjà vu person has no trouble saying NO, no trouble confronting another person and no fear of another's reactions. If we have the courage to upset the right people, we will have little reason to be upset ourselves.

Dr. Cloud follows up on the "9 things" by giving the reader or seeker of wisdom ideas on how to become a Déjà vu person. In this end section, he again discusses the importance of goal setting along with a life-vision. Support groups (like AA or Al-Anon) and Bible studies are helpful. In the program, we call the people in the group "God with Skin." The more books you read (like this one), the more seminars you attend and the more podcasts you listen to will advance your quest and, as Tony Robbins stated in the book reviewed ahead of this one, change your "beliefs" to match what you want to become.

If you can, find role models. My first partner was a great professional role model for me, and I had good friends who were models for me as a husband and parent. In Al-Anon, I have a sponsor whom I meet with on a monthly basis to share intimate thoughts and feelings. Dr. Henry Cloud ends his *9 Things* by encouraging seekers to be patient and persistent (remember my bathroom mirror "P's") and to "Pray, Pray, Pray"!

ENTHUSIASM
NEXT LEVEL THINKING
JOEL OSTEEN

"If you believe you've reached your limits, you have. If you believe you'll never get well, you won't. You have to be bold and get rid of the thoughts that are holding you back."

"If you're letting the odds talk you out of dreaming, out of believing, you're going to miss the fullness of your destiny."

The Fullness of your Destiny is something Joel Osteen talks about in almost every one of the sermons he delivers at Lakewood Church in Houston. His father started the ministry in a humble setting and when he passed many years ago, Joel took up the mantle of pastor and even though not ordained in any denomination his overtly positive message and encouraging and enthusiastic delivery has made him an icon in the televangelism field. Because of his energy and positivity, he took a large church and made it huge by purchasing the Compaq Center, where the Houston Rockets played before building a new coliseum, and then created a television broadcast and wrote many books to reflect the way he views the Christian Message.

The book title reviewed here is *Next Level Thinking*, which captures his overall message that if we remain centered in Christ (God) and his word in the Bible, we will become better people and raise ourselves to the next level in our journey to success and wellbeing. Joel is extremely charismatic, and his constant message of the guarantee of love, success, and better livelihoods obviously resonates with the millions of people who are disciples or at least followers of his TV program, his Sirius radio broadcasts, and his many books.

Joel Osteen is probably the most openly religious sage that I have been influenced by. Of the thirty sages that this writing reviews, I feel that seven are using the teachings and name of Jesus Christ in the writings they have put forth. This 1-to-4 ratio is about right for my journey, in that although I am a Christian I would not call myself religious. When I started my spiritual quest in 1975 in the Al-Anon program, I found the Catholic Church to be an aid in developing my spirituality. I now am a Methodist, but my belief in Jesus Christ as my Higher Power only enhances my understanding of my purpose and growth in a life centered on spirituality. As the last step of the AA and Al-Anon program states: "Having had a spiritual *awakening* as a result of these Steps (in the Al-Anon program), we tried to carry this Message to others, and to practice these principles in all our affairs." The very reason I am writing this book and others is to show how I have been influenced positively and to "carry this Message to others."

There are many Christians and religious preachers and leaders who would reject Joel Osteen's "pie-in-the-sky" philosophy. They would say it is unrealistic and that he is just dangling opportunity and goodwill through TV and radio waves to increase his notoriety and pocketbook. There are many churches who operate on a level of negativity and fear. If you sin, you will be punished—if not in this life, surely in the next. Many churches preach that if your faith in Christ is strong enough, then good things might happen for you. Joel preaches that because you are "a child of the Most High God," good things are bound to happen to you if you maintain a positive belief.

You don't have to be a Christian to know who Joel Osteen is. If you have a radio or TV or occasionally visit the nonfiction section of any bookstore you know who he is, even if you have not heard, seen, or read any of his sermons. My first encounter with him was probably flipping TV channels on a Sunday morning and coming across a young, extremely engaging, and good-looking man preaching to an audience of thousands in a basketball arena. Once you are captured by his enthusiasm you begin to listen to his message, and it is hard not to feel better about yourself and the world when he finishes. He is a little like a young, energetic Norman Vincent Peale, who probably was the first sage to impress me in the 70s.

My two teaching jobs are over two hours away from my home, so I listen to Sirius radio quite a bit. I also have the Audible app from Amazon so I can listen to books on my phone and car. As you can imagine, most of my books and podcasts are self-improvement or spiritually oriented. My habit is downloading a book to listen while I drive but if it ends before I am home or I decide I am not really into it, I automatically turn my radio to Sirius 128 to pick up some "feel-good" lessons from Joel. I also enjoy his call-in live shows and some of the thoughts from guest ministers and personalities. Of all the sages, he is one of the few that keeps motivating me on a weekly basis.

Next Level Thinking is a collection of sermons that Joel has preached from the stage at Lakewood Church in Houston. My thought is that most of his books are taken from his sermons or maybe his sermons were taken from his books. In this book he postulates that each generation gets better or rises to the next level and that is the expectation of God. He is a progressive God and desires every generation to increase.

Like Stephen Covey, Joel believes that comparison and competing are two traits that we are to avoid. In my case, I am not to complain about my height or my age (5'1" and eighty-three, respectively). And I am not to compare myself with others but do the best with what I have been given. God made me small (and let me live to be old), and since he makes no mistakes I need to be grateful for who I am and what I have. As far as competition goes, we are only to compete against ourselves to become the best we can be.

As children, we think that life should be fair but as Reverend Robert Schuller said, "Life isn't fair, but God is good." As long as you are alive, it's because God has something amazing for you to do. If you tend to be critical and negative, don't stay around people who are like that. Find people who are happy, positive, and grateful and follow them. Hurting people hurt people, so be careful who you travel through life with. As long as you're making excuses for where you are you're going to get stuck there, so get up and get out.

Since I once taught Sunday School in the Catholic Church, I used many of the stories of the Old Testament as well as Jesus' teaching in the New Testament. In each chapter of this book and in all of his sermons, Joel uses stories from the Bible to illustrate the principle he is teaching. There is a story in the Old Testament of the prophet Samuel traveling to Bethlehem to seek a suitable young man to be the future king from the house of Jesse. Jesse shows Samuel his son, but Samuel asks if there might be one he didn't see. Jesse says that his youngest, scrawniest, reclusive son named David is with the sheep and when he brings him out to Samuel, the prophet says, "There is the next king." This story shows that no one is too small, weak, or inferior to be exalted in God's kingdom. What Jesse thought of his little son did not affect his future or success. We often rely too much on what people think about us. In the Al-Anon program (and also from Wayne Dyer), we have a slogan that states: "What other people think about me is none of my business."

The story of Moses taking the Hebrews out of Egypt after they were enslaved for so many years is used by the author to show that some people tend to have a "slave mentality." Many of the Hebrews wanted to return to Egypt and resume life as a slave rather than travel through the barren desert with little food and water. Joel says that if you believe the lie that you are a slave, that you've reached your limits, it will keep you from your God-given purpose. One must have an abundance mentality rather than a scarcity or slave outlook on life because you are a child of the Most High God.

In the New Testament, Joel Osteen uses the story about the woman caught in adultery that Jesus saved from stoning and death. Before Jesus talked about her behavior or any of the issues with her accusers, he wanted to make sure she knew she was lovable and loved. After he told her she was not condemned but loved, he then told her to "sin no more." This is an example of "real love." Real love is not about your performance, what you do or don't do. It's about what God has already done.

In a chapter entitled "Approve Yourself," Joel says we are all on the "Potter's Wheel" and are being shaped in the way that brings out the best that God desires.

Joel postulates that while we are being shaped, we make mistakes and have shortcomings. He wants us to look away from our faults and shortcomings because focusing on these negative things will distract us from our purpose. As an All-Anon member who uses the 12 Steps of AA and Al-Anon, I have to disagree a bit with Joel since the 4th Step is "Made a searching and fearless moral inventory of ourselves." In this step we acknowledge our shortcomings, which enables us to learn how to minimize them. We also learn about the good character traits we have, and in the 5th Step we admit this all to "God, ourselves, and another human being," which enables us to overcome these defects with the help of program people and our Higher Power (God).

In another chapter, Joel emphasizes that what you are going through at present may not be good, but God knows how to bring good out of it. In the program of Al-Anon we have another saying: "If it's not good, it may be for your good." This means that we often do things or want to do things that we think would benefit us or be the right move. When we do them, they don't turn out like we hoped they would and that may be because our Higher Power or God knows that this would be a move that would not be best and may even be quite harmful.

One of the worst emotions we can carry is "bitterness." The answer is forgiveness, and we must learn how to do that unconditionally. God not only forgives us our trespasses, but he even forgets them. On the other hand, when we forgive remembering how we were offended or wounded is a good idea so we don't fall back into the same situation again.

In many of his sermons and writings, Joel Osteen talks about overcoming the difficult issues and faulty directions of our lives. He always mentions addiction as one of those negative paths we sometimes take and tells the reader that they are NOT addicts! He feels they are Children of God with an addiction and shouldn't be labeled as an addict. He may be semantically right since addiction is a disease, but when a man or woman gets up in front of the room at an AA meeting and says, "Hi, I'm Shirley, alcoholic," it has a lasting effect. The fact that they label themselves that way seems to make it easier for them to abstain and recover.

In the Big Book of AA, Bill Wilson says that it is rare that the alcoholic resumes drinking if he or she follow the Steps and the principles of the program. However, he emphasizes that it takes "rigorous honesty and there are some poor unfortunates" that seem unable to be honest at that level. Joel believes that real healing begins when we get honest. He also feels you will need to find a person of integrity whom you can trust to walk with you through whatever you are dealing with. In the AA and Al-Anon program this is a sponsor, and this trusted person helps you "work" the Steps, especially the 4th and 5th, where you have to take a personal inventory and then relate your findings to another human being.

All of Joel's sermons at Lakewood end the exact same way with the exact same words, and he ends his book in similar fashion:

"Would you pray with me today? Just say: 'Lord Jesus, I repent of my sins, I ask You to come into my heart. I make you my Lord and Savior.' Friend, if you prayed that simple prayer, I believe you have been 'born again.' I encourage you to attend a good Bible-based church and keep God first place in your life."

ACCEPTANCE
THE GIFTS OF IMPERFECTION
BRENE BROWN

"How much we know and understand ourselves is critically important, but there is something that is even more essential to living a wholehearted life: loving ourselves."

"We are biologically, cognitively, physically, and spiritually wired to love, to be loved, and to belong."

There are basically three things we must accept in life. In no particular order, they are UNCERTAINTY, IMPERMANENCE, and IMPERFECTION. Nothing is ever certain "except death and taxes," and taxes are really not that certain depending on where you live and how much you make. Uncertainty not only makes life challenging but also exciting. It would not be good to be sure of the outcome of everything we say, do, or attempt. We know that all things are not permanent. The saying "This too shall pass" is a direct reference to that fact. The good things will wane or disappear, and the bad things will end and be relegated to the past. The closing of each Al-Anon meeting has a paragraph, which states: "We aren't perfect. The welcome we give you may not show the warmth we have in our hearts for you. After a while, you'll discover that though you may not like all of us, you'll love us in a very special way—the same way we already love you." Imperfection is inherent in every individual. Another Al-Anon slogan reminds us to seek "Progress over Perfection." Only God is perfect, and the book written by Brene Brown tells us that imperfection is a gift. We only get into deep trouble when we try to achieve perfection.

At the start of my journey in using the works of the sages to develop an elevated character, I was mostly interested in a more spiritual quest. The program of Al-Anon that fueled my need to improve was a spiritual program and the Steps were in place to create a "Spiritual Experience" that would make me a better father, spouse, friend, and orthodontist. Somewhere in the midst of that journey, I became interested in authors and personalities that could influence my psychological and emotional wellbeing. Brene Brown was one of those authors. The book of hers I chose to take material from is a ten-year update on *The Gifts of Imperfection* that was widely acclaimed when it first came out.

Brene is a "shame researcher" and contends that all of us have been shamed or felt ashamed at some time in our lives. Her definition of shame is "the fear of being unlovable." My definition is that you believe you are defective, bad, and unworthy. It is differentiated from guilt in that with guilt you DID something bad or wrong, and with shame you ARE something bad or wrong. With guilt you can make amends or apologize, but shame is more of a stigma that doesn't disappear even when you apologize or make amends. I never considered myself as feeling shameful but after reading *The Gifts of Imperfection*, I believe as Brene does that we all have felt shame in our lives at some time.

Brene Brown is also a recovering alcoholic who has been sober since 1996. Maybe this is why I not only learned from her writings but felt a certain bond in her spiritual search. Her book doesn't dwell on God very much, but she feels that a connection to a Higher Power is necessary for spiritual health and development. In times of stress and uncertainty, she uses the Serenity Prayer from the AA program to gain perspective and peace. She does not seem to participate in AA meetings and does not talk about the Steps. She also agrees with Joel Osteen that saying "Hi, I'm Brene, alcoholic" is disempowering, so even though she acknowledges the disease she would rather learn from it than embrace it.

Besides teaching people how to overcome shame and the need to be perfect, the goal in this writing is to be able to create a pattern of WHOLE-HEARTED LIVING.

There are ten Guideposts to achieving that state and each guidepost is thoroughly discussed with guides on implementation. Before discussing the Guideposts, the three "Gifts of Imperfection" are COURAGE, COMPASSION, AND CONNECTION. Stephen Covey had the "Four C's" and now Brene gives us her "Three C's." The first gift is courage, which is speaking honestly and openly about who we are, about what we are feeling, and about our experiences, both good and bad. It is the ability to be vulnerable and put ourselves out there to others even when we are a bit fearful.

With courage we say, "What others think about me is none of my business."

I have a lecture that I give each year to the residents at the two orthodontic schools where I teach called "Professional Pitfalls - Sh*t Happens!" I review seven or eight cases where I was either sued or nearly sued or where treatment went off the rails. The first time I gave this lecture, I was afraid the residents would think I wasn't a very good orthodontist and they would think less of me because of my "failings." My surprise was that they respected me more for addressing this delicate topic and giving them advanced warning about what could go wrong and cause a lawsuit.

The second "C" or second Gift of Imperfection is Compassion. This gift is the ability to suffer with another, which is not the default mode for most of us. We feel sorry for the person's suffering but are slow to jump in and share it with them. I blame my father for my lack of compassion. I think most of us blame our parents for our tendencies whether it is true or not. My father was a stoic. He was very calm at all times and very distant when another was hurting or in trouble. Very little emotion or compassion, as I recall. If compassion is inherited, I can blame my lack of compassion on him. My wife was the most compassionate person I ever knew. If you were doing well she had little time for you, but if you were hurting in some way she was there for you as long as it took.

Compassion requires us to have boundaries. We show compassion even when we tell someone no and when we confront them for their own good. The compassionate person does this firmly and calmly but also without berating them or putting them down. Kindness is an integral part of being compassionate.

The third and last gift of imperfection and third "C" is Connection. To belong and connect properly, we have to eliminate Stephen Covey's "Four Harmful C's": Complaining, Comparing, Criticizing and Competing. We must relish the vulnerability in belonging. As a part of belonging, all people get energy when they are in a relationship where they feel seen, heard, and valued. Belonging is more than just having your name on the roster of a group and fitting in. Because we realize our imperfection, we must be able to ask for and accept help from others. This is definitely one of my weaknesses and

I won't blame it on my parents. The Al-Anon program has taught me to ask for help, especially with the alcoholics in my life, but I have to overcome years of thinking everything was up to me to handle without outside help. This is obviously very ego-based, and I not only receive help weekly from my Al-Anon sponsor and friends but also my Higher Power or the God of my understanding.

THE TEN GUIDEPOSTS
TO ACHIEVE
WHOLEHEARTED LIVING

AUTHENTICITY

As Brene describes it, authenticity is the daily practice of letting go of who we think we are supposed to be and embracing who we really are. For an Approval Addict like myself, that is a difficult challenge. I have always been a "people pleaser" and in order to "look good" or "get people to like and appreciate me," I had to play a role that often was not authentic. Here is where the gift of imperfection comes in. Authentic behavior and authentic people are not afraid to show that they are flawed or imperfect because they have the courage to express their true nature and not be concerned about what other people think about them. In Al-Anon we have the "Q-TIP" slogan, which is short for "Quit Taking It Personally." People with the courage to be authentic are aware that other people's responses to what we do and say is up to them and not us.

SELF-COMPASSION

Overcoming shame is the quickest way to self-compassion because shame is the birthplace of perfectionism. In order to be kind to ourselves, we must get over the fear of making mistakes, failing, and disappointing others. This second guidepost is where Brene uses the Serenity Prayer extensively. She (and we) pray for Acceptance, Courage, and Wisdom to move forward with regard to self-care. One of my five strongest character defects is judgment. When we practice self-compassion, we are careful not to judge ourselves as well as other people. The self-compassionate individual knows that just showing up is enough!

RESILIENCE

Resilience is the ability to overcome adversity. Here, Brene and I agree that spirituality is definitely necessary for resilience. The opposite of resilience is hopelessness and when I first came into the Al-Anon program, I had no hope. My marriage was over, my life was spiraling down and by the grace of God, I was led to a program that could restore my faith in God and lead me out of the dark pit of hopelessness I found myself in. The Second Step of AA and Al-Anon is the step of Hope. "We came to believe that a Power greater than ourselves could lead us to sanity." My distant relationship with any power other than myself created my hopelessness. In order to gain hope and confidence that "it will be okay," I had to realize that it was not up to me alone to do it. I could develop a relationship with God that would give me confidence and hope that would help pull me out of the pit of adversity. The fellow members of the Al-Anon group or the "God with Skin" helped with support and strength, and got me out of the habit of not asking others for help.

GRATITUDE AND JOY

Gratitude is the antidote to many of our behavioral ills. Two of my biggest ones are self-pity and negativity. When I get in these moods, I have to remind myself of everything I have in life, and I have to do it right there on the spot. My prayers usually start with thanking God for my health, my lifestyle, my lack of financial worry, my healthy children and grandchild, and that I can still teach and volunteer in a hospital at my age. In our Saturday Al-Anon meeting, we had the "Gratitude Queen" Billie, an octogenarian who couldn't walk, had weekly dialysis for kidney issues, carried an oxygen machine with nasal canula and oozed gratitude despite her health concerns. What a great example for all of us. I have tried to journal off and on over the years, and when I do I always finish with my "top ten" items to be grateful for. This also helps me get over my awful habit of complaining (to myself) and not being content with where I am with what I have. Joy is a bit harder to capture than gratitude. One author describes it as "a light that fills you with hope, faith, and love." Happiness is tied to circumstance and joyfulness is tied to spirit and gratitude. Scarcity is the enemy of joy and gratitude. We can have a feeling of overall joy and well-being when we know that there is always enough, and we are always enough.

INTUITION AND TRUSTING FAITH

When we started discussing the lessons learned in this book, we talked about UNCERTAINTY. The research done by Brene Brown for this book shows that what silences our inner or intuitive voice is our need for certainty. Our intuition seems to direct us in a positive path, but we ignore that "small still voice" because we are uncertain about the outcome. A slogan I developed in the Al-Anon program that I call my "Nike" slogan reads: "Just do it, and detach from the outcome!" We cannot control how events turn out, but we also cannot allow our fear of negative outcomes to stifle our action. One of the sages we reviewed, Andy Andrews, reminds us that the two most important words in his book and maybe in our lives is to "DO SOMETHING!" Like me, Brene does not believe that faith means "everything happens for a reason." Both of us are not comfortable using God, faith, or spirituality to explain tragedy. My best friend in Al-Anon was the kindest, gentlest man on the planet and he was better at welcoming newcomers to the program than any man ever was. His life ended tragically last summer by a drunk driver. He had a purpose on this planet, and I will never believe there was a "reason" for the car accident and his death. The third Step of AA and Al-Anon cements my faith and the ability to trust in God. In this Step, we "make a decision to turn our life and will over to the care of God," even with the uncertainty that this entails.

CREATIVITY

You may not like my writing and if so you are not even reading this. However, it is one of the ways I express my creativity. I am creating something even if it's only for my own good and not that of the universe. I have written three books so far and none of my children or relatives have read any of them. I also teach, which requires creativity, and read to kids in a children's hospital. I do not dance, draw, take pictures (well), knit, paint, sculpt or cook.

There are no humans without creativity. However, there are many people who do not use their creativity. Again, we often do not use our creativity because of fear of not being "perfect" or not being appreciated for our talent or lack of talent. Another problem that stifles creativity is the bad habit of COMPARISON and COMPETITION. These two of Stephen Covey's undesirable "C's" pop up again and again in keeping us held back and held down. We are afraid our creative work will not compare well with that of others who we are thought to be in competition with. We need to remove concepts like ahead or behind as well as best or worst.

PLAY AND REST

These two qualities ebb and flow all throughout one's life. My one-year-old grandson plays for twelve hours and rests for twelve hours. As we age, we tend to play less and that really is a tragedy. However, we tend to rest more and that is usually good. Like all of life, BALANCE is the key and getting adequate amounts of play and rest. I am not a spontaneous person who plays on a moment's notice and takes power naps during the day. I have always had a "plan" for the day and often forget to program in periods of play and rest even though they are extremely important in creating a wholehearted existence. I used to play racquetball and I love to kayak and bicycle. I want to learn to play pickleball but am not sure I can, as I have had five surgeries on my left leg and two on my right. I have always wanted to have a playful demeanor, but that is not my nature. Those of us who have "Daily Lists" need to learn to put them away for a day or make sure to put "play and rest" on that list.

CALM AND STILLNESS

The Eleventh Step of AA and Al-Anon states: "Sought through PRAYER and MEDITATION to improve our conscious contact with God as I understand Him, praying only for knowledge of His will for us and the power to carry it out." Daily prayer (all day) and morning meditation are the best way in my mind to create calm and stillness. You have to program it into your day, or at least I do. Every morning that I am home, I read the page for the day in my three "daily readers" from Al-Anon. I also read the page for the day in the "Daily Word" from Unity and a chapter in the Message, the contemporary Bible. I have the *Calm* app on my phone, and I go through two daily meditations with Jay Shetty and Tamara Levitt. I pray often when I am driving to my two distant teaching jobs (two and a half hours of travel). The meditation practice has taught me to program DEEP BREATHING into my prayer and meditation, which helps. Another thing that helps is that I live alone and am "retired." Sometimes the stillness becomes a negative but then I can turn to my quest for creativity and fun.

MEANINGFUL WORK

When I attended seminars on retirement years ago, they would always advise the participants, "Retire to something, not from something!" I knew when I retired I would have to do something meaningful. After forty-six years of creating ideal occlusions and smiles with orthodontics and ensuring positive careers and relationships for my patients, I knew I had to contribute to the world on the highest level possible to feel worthwhile and fulfilled. Brene Brown might tell me that I don't need job fulfillment to feel good about myself, I'm good enough just being me. However, my two teaching jobs and the forty-two young dentists that I mentor fulfill my feeling of "purpose" and I do not plan to retire from that. Helping newcomers in the Al-Anon program and sponsoring a young man also is rewarding, hopefully for both of us. Volunteering in a children's hospital is also more rewarding to me than to the kids I read to. I very much agree with Brene that God lives in us, not above us. Sharing our gifts with the world is the most powerful source of connection with God. We are advised to refuse to be defined by a single career and rather than asking what the world needs, we are to ask, "What makes us come alive?"

LAUGHTER, SONG, AND DANCE

My aversion to dancing has already been mentioned. My wife hated dancing, so we never went to dances and now my dancing legs are bad, and I have no one to dance with. I sang in my high school octet and numerous church choirs and glee clubs over the years, but my voice has lowered and become gravely so I either rarely sing or sing quietly so no one hears me. I am trying to laugh at myself more rather than taking everything that happens so seriously. My default mode is to berate myself when I do something I shouldn't have rather than to just laugh it off. When I fall off my bike or knock my cereal bowl on the floor, I am trying to laugh at myself or say softly, "Isn't that interesting?" rather than "How could I be so clumsy or stupid?" Laughter not only combats negativity but reduces the severity and seriousness of most of our daily untoward occurrences. Laughing at ourselves gives us permission to be free and when we can't do this, we rarely tolerate that freedom in others.

We are to practice the TEN GUIDEPOSTS OF WHOLEHEARTED LIVING daily to become all that God intended us to be. Although Brene did not regularly attend AA meetings, she had an AA friend who heard a behavioral reminder at an AA meeting called a Vowel Check – AEIOU:

A – Have I been *ABSTINENT* today? If you're not an alcoholic, put something else you are addicted to in its place.

E – Have I *EXERCISED* today?

I – What have *I* done for myself today?

O – What have I done for *OTHERS* today?

U – Am I holding onto *UNEXPRESSED* emotions today?

Y – *YEAH!* What is something good that is happening today?

PURPOSE
START WITH WHY
SIMON SINEK

"Achievement comes when you pursue and attain WHAT you want. Success comes when you are clear in pursuit of WHY you want it."

"To inspire people to do the things that inspired them, so that, together, we can change the world. That's the path to which my life and my work is now completely devoted."

In my quest to become "spiritually awakened," the sages I read and listened to were chosen to bring me closer to God with principles and practices that lifted the soul and made me a better citizen of the world. However, when you are on a self-improvement quest and you are the leader of a business, you may discover writers who move you to a higher plane in your chosen profession. Simon Sinek's concept of running an organization or business by discovering WHY you are in business in the first place is an example. Nowhere in his featured book *Start with Why* does he mention God or Spirit or prayer or even meditation. But his philosophy is one in which the God of my Understanding would heartily approve of.

For forty-six years, I was the leader or coleader of an orthodontic practice. In order to be successful, I had to know how to run that business, so it was profitable and properly served the community I lived in. Professionals in medicine and dentistry require so much schooling in diagnosis and treatment of human physical problems that they do not get much instruction on the principles of running a successful business. I know quite a few dentists who were excellent clinicians, but their practice failed because they didn't employ successful business principles. In the two schools where I am a clinical instructor,

I give a lecture on "Orthobusiness" because the school does not offer them anything in that important realm.

The American Association of Orthodontists has contracted with the Wharton School of Business so its members can take a course that will help them survive and achieve in the business world.

Simon Sinek informs us in his book that the leaders of businesses have to be "Visionaries." Their goal must be to "Inspire" the people in the organization and the clients who would do business with them. And the only way to inspire them is to be sure of WHY you are in business. Your employees and the people who "buy" from you have to know your WHY and believe in it themselves for you to be successful over a very long term. With a clear-cut WHY you are in business, you breed loyalty and long-term business and success.

Many companies use "manipulation" rather than a clear sense of purpose. They use price by lowering it for the consumer or raising salaries for the employees but that does not breed loyalty. Fear is another "motivator"—"if you don't buy my product or service you will get sick, not be able to eat, get fat, or it will be sold out." Manipulation works in that you get business but not loyalty or a belief that you are worthy of people's trust.

Many business leaders will tell you that MONEY is WHY you work or run a business. But money is just a measure of "how you are growing or shrinking" and not an indicator of long-term success.

Sinek lists numerous well-known companies that have purposes that attract people and convert them into ambassadors no matter the cost or convenience. The company mentioned the most is Apple, whose WHY is to "challenge the status quo." They are constantly innovating and taking risks with new products and services, but the products have nothing to do with their WHY, they are just a result of constantly pressing the limit of innovation. Another company mentioned along with Apple is Harley Davidson, whose loyal "subjects" even tattoo the company logo on arms and legs. People he lists as visionaries rather than salesmen are the Wright Brothers, Martin Luther King, Ronald Reagan, and John Kennedy.

Until I heard Simon Sinek's TED talk or read his books, I thought the WHY of my business was to "straighten crooked teeth." But I quickly learned that tooth alignment was WHAT I did, not my WHY. Sinek's "GOLDEN CIRCLE" has three concentric rings with the WHY on the inside because it's the most important. In the next outer ring is HOW you achieve your why. In my cases, it would be stainless-steel braces or plastic aligners. In the outer ring or circle orbiting the other two is the WHAT. It's here we find the goal of straightening teeth and optimizing faces and appearance. As you will notice, production and profitability are nowhere in the circle. If you get the WHY right, the profit will take care of itself!

So now I have to find my WHY! It is to "create optimum futures." This works for both my patients and employees. Having a well-aligned jaw structure and an engaging and attractive smile will ensure future job prospects and enhance relationship possibilities. So the improved success of my patients in the future is WHY I am doing WHAT I do. I also want my employees to feel a part of that outreach and treat them and pay them well to create an optimum future for them as well.

The important point is that those that believe in and share our WHY will also TRUST us. The limbic system in the brain is in the emotional mid-brain, where gut reaction occurs. People who relate to your WHY are drawn to you by emotion. If consumers or employees do not buy into your WHY, they need to use the neo-cortex of the outer brain to make decisions and this "thinking" process rather than emotional reacting makes them less likely to believe, trust and be loyal. Because of this "gut loyalty," businesses with a clearly established WHY attract people who are innovators or "early adopters," which are only about 15 to 18 percent of the population but are very loyal and very likely to act upon your product. They do not respond to "features and benefits" of WHAT you do but make the gut choice to remain loyal, even if they can get the WHAT for less money.

Simon Sinek discusses the importance of proper hiring. Obviously, the prospective employee needs to know and believe in your WHY. They must understand that self-gain or wealth is not the objective. We should hire attitude and not skill, which can be taught. In my practice, for instance, the clinical assistants must understand that we are working TOWARD successful futures for the patient and not just working ON the patient's teeth and face. One of the principles that I have emphasized on reviewing all of the sages is the value of LISTENING. Again, this is promoted by Simon Sinek in relation to book clients and people working in your organization.

Dr. Seuss is one of my favorite authors. One of his stories, "The Sneetches," is paraphrased in Sinek's book, to my delight. I read that story to children in Akron Children's Hospital, where I volunteer as a "Roving Reader" on Wednesday mornings. It is a story about a tribe of weird beings that live on a beach. Half have stars on their bellies and the other half "have none upon thars." Of course, the ones without stars are ostracized by the ones who have stars, and it takes a shrewd businessman, Sylvester McMoney McBean, to offer to give the starless Snitches what they long for on their bellies. It is a story of BELONGING and Sinek says that is a motivator for loyal devotees of Apple and your company. We all want to belong and be a part of something large and significant.

Sinek discusses something he calls "The Celery Test." If you offer a consumer a series of products such as a pack of M&Ms, a bagel, prime rib, or a latte from Starbucks, and a celery stick, which would they choose? The missing link is that you have no idea what the motivation for the consumer is. WHAT is he looking for and WHY? If it turns out that he is concerned about health, then you know that he will choose the celery and turn down the other products.

Even though this book is basically one for business, the overriding principles are definitely spiritual. We are to lead by lifting up those in our organization as well as listen to them intently. We are to discount competition with others with our objective being to be better today than we were yesterday. In doing this, our goal is to attain our WHY and improve the community and world.

RISK

THE 5 SECOND RULE
MEL ROBBINS

"Change comes down to the courage you need to make five second decisions."

"One moment of courage can change your day. One day can change your life. And your life can change the world."

The second quote comes from the last page of Mel Robbins' book, and it sums up the whole essence of the message she is presenting. The motivational speaker, author, and daytime talk show host has written this book to promote the concept of COURAGE. There are many things we would like to do and even many things we should do or even have to do that we do not do. It takes courage to do many things in life and Mel Robbins has found out that the "five second rule" will help override hesitation and prompt the ACTION that one has been putting off or avoiding.

In 2009, the author witnessed a televised rocket launch and the countdown to blastoff struck a chord and gave her an idea to prompt action. She decided to have a five-second countdown like they do in the space program and then "blast off" or "act" on whatever it was she was contemplating on doing that should be done. The first thing she used this on was getting out of bed in the morning. Instead of hitting the snooze button, she started counting backwards, starting at five—"5, 4, 3, 2, 1—Blastoff!"—(rip off the covers and hop out of bed).

As she used this little prompt in other things in her life, she began to make changes that turned things around with her marriage, other relationships, and her career. Like many of the sages that are being reviewed, she had an issue with alcohol or chemicals and was able to overcome them with this "Rule." It only works if you count DOWN to blastoff and not up to nothing. You can start with a higher number than five or a lesser number, but five seconds is her recommendation.

Besides examples of how the "Rule" has helped in her life, the book is full of emails, texts, Tweets, and social media posts from people who heard her TED talk or heard her at a seminar, thanking her for giving them this simple tool that enabled them to move forward in life with things that they wanted or needed to do but were unable until they "counted down to blastoff." Many people were able to quit their jobs, leave marriages, move across the country, backpack in the Andes, dance at weddings, start a company, retire, get married, say no to a significant other, and make many other changes that they had been putting off.

Most of the chapters of the book have the word COURAGE in the heading somewhere. Courage to "act NOW" promotes the needed action, which in turn builds CONFIDENCE. Mel uses the term "Real Confidence," and this makes the next needed action easier and more likely to be carried out. *The 5 Second Rule* is used to make decisions, ask for help, speak up to people one needs or wants to speak to and overcome procrastination. The book points out that the inner wisdom we use to make the decision to act doesn't come from "feelings." If we rely on how we feel, we will never act. Immediate action comes from the prefrontal cortex and overcomes the immediate feeling of fear.

When we reviewed Stephen Covey's *7 Habits*, we found out that the first habit was "BE PROACTIVE." That's exactly what we do when we take the five-second countdown and act immediately. In the book reviewed by Andy Andrews, *The Traveler's Summit*, we found that the two-word slogan that would "save the world" was "DO SOMETHING!" In other words, ACT NOW. Again, this is the whole essence of this habit of reverse counting and immediate action.

Mel Robbins discusses the "adverse habits" that we create over time. Patterns of thinking, like worrying, self-doubt, and fear, are all just habits—and you repeat these patterns of thinking and behaving without even realizing it. She lists these habits (page 59) as Waiting, Doubting, Holding Back, Staying Silent, Feeling Insecure, Avoiding, Worry, and Overthinking. All the above "Habits" that she outlines come from one trait: FEAR. We get into a mode of hesitation when we fear that acting will create an adverse consequence rather than a beneficial one. Two of the fears most of us have quite often are Fear of Rejection and Fear of Uncertainty. The fear of failure can be categorized under the fear of both rejection and uncertainty. As hockey great Wayne Gretzky commented on why he took so many shots, "You miss 100 percent of the shots you don't take!" We only have one life or one "shot," so using the five-second rule to take that shot in many areas of our lives makes a lot of sense. Pema Chodron is one of the sages we still have to cover, and she discusses fully the Fear of Uncertainty. When we act, we never really know the consequences of that action. Every outcome is uncertain, and we must move ahead without obsessing on the result of our action. Hopefully, you will remember the quote I came up with: "Just do it, and detach from the outcome."

The 5 Second Rule helps a person with the habit of procrastination. People put off doing what must or should be done to avoid stress. Perfectionists tend to procrastinate because they are afraid the decision they make or act they take will not come out ideally. The Al-Anon slogan "Progress, not Perfection" reminds us that we just need to move forward toward the goal, not obsess on whether we achieve it or not.

Mel Robbins feels that the first three hours in the morning, from 6:30 A.M. to 9:30 A.M., are when you are most likely to act and accomplish your goals. It helps to create a daily routine during that time, which includes spiritual reading, meditation, and planning. Like Mel, I think this is essential. When I had an active practice, I would get up at 5:00 A.M., get to the YMCA for an hour of exercise until 6:30, go across the street from the Y to St. Paul's Church, where I would pray and meditate (no service at that hour), and then get to the office by 7:30 to plan the day and get ready for patients. Now that I am retired, I get up at 6 or 7 and read the Daily Word from Unity, a page from *Quiet Times with God* by Joyce Meyer, the daily page from my three Al-Anon readers—"One Day at a Time," "Courage to Change," and "Hope for Today"—a chapter from the Bible, and then meditate for twenty minutes using the *Calm* app on my phone.

In full disclosure, I have not used the "5 Second Rule" other than to think about it when I know I need to act. Mel Robbins started using the rule to get out of bed in the morning and not press the snooze button. I have never used the snooze button and have never had trouble getting out of bed. During my married years, my biggest challenge in carrying out prompt action was when I should be telling people what I wanted and how I felt. As an "Approval Addict" and conflict avoider, I didn't want to create a crisis or risk losing a relationship so I remained silent when I should have "5, 4, 3, 2, 1, Blasted off (Say it!)!" Fear of rejection and abandonment have played a large role in my life, probably because I grew up in an alcoholic household and was an only child.

I once was upset with my practice partner because he wouldn't let me make improvements to the practice that I thought were necessary. I was planning to leave him and the practice when a man in my Friday morning Bible study said, "Have you talked to him about it yet?" Of course I hadn't, and when I realized this was the practical and right thing to do I didn't use the "5 Second Rule" when I entered his office but did open the door and hesitate a second to let God walk in ahead of me to provide my courage. Of course he welcomed my input, said the changes I had made so far had upgraded the practice and gave me carte blanche to act as I saw fit. I never had to leave him and find another practice.

As I indicated in the above paragraphs in reference to my wife and my business partner, the courage to act is most imperative in one's relationships. Both Mel Robbins and I agree, Intimacy takes courage. The sage and author sums up the need for the courage to act near the end of the book when she says "Do not leave anything unsaid" in your relationships. When in doubt, count backwards from five and "SAY IT."

Mel Robbins has a similar book out that I listened to on my Audible app while I drove to my two distant teaching jobs in Ohio and Pennsylvania. The "High-Five Habit" is a little like the "5 Second Rule" except it is an action rather than a countdown. Both can be done in a few seconds, and both generate a promotion of energy, proactivity, and positivity in the moment. With the High-Five Habit, one tapes an outline of your own hand on the bathroom mirror and then when you get up (using the 5 Second Rule) you immediately go into the bathroom and place your hand on the cutout hand tapped to the mirror and "give yourself a high-five" to start the day. It also helps if you have an affirmation typed on the cutout paper mirror hand. Mine reads: "Everything about me is loveable and worthy of love!" Do I use it every day? Like the "5 Second Rule," I see it, I think about it, and it helps me remember to summon the courage to act in a positive and constructive way.

FREEDOM
THE UNTETHERED SOUL
MICHAEL SINGER

"The truth is, everything will be okay as soon as you are okay with everything."

"Deep inner release is a spiritual path in and of itself. It is the path of NONRESISTANCE, the path of ACCEPTANCE, the path of SURRENDER" (caps mine).

After being a member of Al-Anon for forty-eight years and attending at least one meeting a week for that length of time, I could define the program in one word: SURRENDER! The accompanying term I would use would be HUMILITY, but it takes the utmost humility to surrender so I like the idea of surrender as being the ultimate goal of the membership.

When you live with an alcoholic or problem drinker, the problem becomes yours. Al-Anon teaches that it is not your problem to solve and that you really cannot actually solve it, and efforts to do so often make the problem worse and increase your angst and unhappiness. You must be willing to surrender to the disease of alcoholism or chemical dependency and accept that you are powerless to make a definitive change in another person. You must learn that it is not your responsibility and also that it is frustrating because it is futile.

Michael Singer's short book teaches that the path to ultimate spirituality, which includes enthusiasm, love, and joy, comes by not only accepting what is or has happened but being okay with it. Being able to "let go" of events, whether positive or negative, is the key to happiness and fulfillment. Personal and spiritual growth comes from accepting and transcending the part of you that is not okay and needs protection.

The book opens with the author discussing the "voice" we have that talks incessantly to us. He calls this our "roommate" because the discussion goes on endlessly when we are alone. He maintains that the voice is not you, the true you only hears the voice and decides on what to do about it. Interestingly Eckhart Tolle, whom we reviewed earlier, also talks about people "talking to themselves" when they already know what they are experiencing without the need to verbalize it out loud or in their mind. Too often, our "roommate" or inner voice is discussing things that are negative or things we need to fear or look out for, and this can cause us spiritual harm if we follow the wrong line of thought.

We all have infinite energy, and this energy is enhanced by accepting what is and being okay with it rather than being discontented or upset with it. Our mind and especially our heart is open to energy when we are accepting and positive and are able to let go and our mind and heart closes when we fear or need protection. Energy needs openness and receptivity so the spiritual goal is to stay open and never close. This is the source of the light and an open heart leads to enthusiasm, joy, and love. He uses the Sanskrit word "Samskara" to define the blockage of energy or things that cause the heart to close. Again, he mentions clinging to things, pushing things away, and seeking protection as energy drainers or blockers, and one achieves liberation by not protecting and just LETTING GO.

Returning to the Al-Anon program, which closely follows Singer's spiritual philosophy, we let go by DETACHING. We accept occurrences and people as they are and detach from the desire to change them in any way. We detach from challenging them on their behavior and offering them advice on how to behave and act. We do not get angry with them but leave them alone and prevent an altercation by removing ourselves emotionally and maybe even physically. In the Al-Anon program, we follow the 12 Steps of AA and Al-Anon and the Third Step tells us to "Make a decision to turn our lives and our wills over to the care of God as we understand Him." Thus, we "turn the person or people who offend us over to the God of their understanding" and LET GO. The slogan we use to remind us of this practice is "LET GO AND LET GOD." If you have been in the program for as long as I have, you start to make up your own slogans. One of my slogans that follows the premise of Michael Singer's book is "ACCEPT, SURRENDER, LET GO" (LET GOD). Our spirituality suffers and our heart closes when we do not have the courage to act when necessary and let fear hold us back.

The members of Al-Anon have a disease just like the alcoholic or addicted person. Our disease is one of CONTROL. We feel the need to have everything and everyone under our control and will stop at nothing until we feel things are going the exact way we want them to. It has been said by addiction-ologists (doctors who treat alcoholics) that all of us have a "hole in our soul." Religious people will say we have a "God Hole." The addict fills that "hole" with the drug or chemical of their choice, whereas the Al-Anon member or codependent fills it with trying to control everything in their lives.

Alcohol was important to me when I was in my twenties and thirties. My wife's drinking was one of the things that attracted me to her. But when her drinking became problematic, I tried turning to alcohol myself as a refuge. But every time I went to my favorite bar to drown my troubles, I would think of my wife back in the apartment using while taking care of my one-year-old son. That image would immediately cause me to shove my beer away and race out to my car so I could get home and control the situation. My "disease" was defined early on in my marriage.

Michael Singer indicates that FEAR is the cause of every problem. Problems such as self-consciousness, jealousy, anxiety, and insecurity are all outward manifestations of fear.

A spiritual writing called *A Course in Miracles* states that there are really only two emotions in human behavior. All the good, positive emotions come out of LOVE and all the negative ones, including anger, resentment, and even violence, come from FEAR. Fear is the reason that we have more guns in the United States than people!

People on the lower rungs of spirituality have a "thorn" in their bodies. The thorn may be loneliness, rejection, appearance (in my case age and height). Singer explains that the thorn can be "covered" so it doesn't poke you, but it still exists. The only true and long-lasting remedy is to remove the thorn. Like having a thorn in our skin, we will have pain in our lives. The author teaches us that we should not avoid the pain but learn to accept it as a part of life. We are to lower our expectations of a pain-free existence and learn to "Relax and Release."

One of the philosophies that the author refers to in one chapter is "The Tao Te Ching." If you have read about an earlier sage, Wayne Dyer, you will recall that the book of his I used was all on the teaching of the Tao for modern times. Singer uses this ancient Chinese philosophy to indicate that spiritually evolved people are in BALANCE as the Tao advances. One should be "in the middle" in all things, never running too hot or too cold. Avoid compulsive behavior on both ends.

Two behavior patterns that the spiritually enlightened person avoids are DEFENDING and JUDGING. You must learn to be comfortable with psychological disturbance. Many of our elected politicians are moving away from spirituality rather than toward it. They are not only continually defending themselves and their ways of thinking but seem to think that judging others is their job. Not to mention calling others names and minimizing the truth!

Actually, when you really are on the path to spiritualty you are totally different from everybody else. That which everybody else wants, you don't want. That which everybody else resists, you totally accept. This is the path of NON-RESISTANCE to what is and is the key to being happy. We are told to be happy no matter what happens. A slogan that refers to this that I heard in an AA talk years ago is "Would you rather be happy or would you rather be right?"

In many books about personal growth or spiritual growth, there is little talk about God.

Michael Singer finishes his book with a chapter called "The Loving Eyes of God." He firmly believes that deep within us there is a direct connection to the Divine, which he calls God. This connection is where LOVE comes in. Many religious people believe that only God can judge, but Singer is so opposed to the idea of judging others that he states that God is pure love rather than a judging ruler. No matter what you do or what you have done, you will always be totally loved by Him.

My recovery in Al-Anon could not have happened without a Higher Power, whom I call God. An addict cannot recover without the prayerful Hope in God, and neither can a control freak. Once you have a firm belief and an overwhelming trust in God, you lose anxiety and tension. You can feel love, sometimes for no reason. Your backdrop is love. Your backdrop is openness, beauty, and gratitude.

To somewhat meld religion and spirituality, Singer takes several quotes from the Gospel of John, where Jesus teaches his followers that "I and my Father are One" and God or the Divine or Spirit is in us as well. Just as we receive a single ray from the sun, that ray is just as much the sun as the bright orange ball in the sky. To sum up this book, the AA and Al-Anon slogan "LET GO, LET GOD" is very much appropriate.

CHANGE
LIVING BEAUTIFULLY
PEMA CHODRON

"Rather than living a life of resistance and trying to disprove our basic situation of IMPERMANANCE and CHANGE, we could contact the fundamental ambiguity and welcome it!"

"Awakening is not a process of building ourselves up but a process of LETTING GO."

*L*iving Beautifully is the 27th of the thirty spiritual books I promised to review. It exemplifies my movement from pure religion into the more spiritual realm of many worldly practices. The previously reviewed book by Michael Singer is very similar in concept and teaching to this book by the Buddhist nun Pema Chodron. Singer does refer quite a bit to Biblical teaching of Jesus in the later pages of his book but as a Buddhist, Chodron does not mention Biblical teachings or Christianity. In fact, she makes it clear that there is "no true way" and professes that many religious practices are off base in trying to promote "the way" or specifically "their way."

Several things are absolute. They are UNCERTAINTY, IMPERMANANCE, and CHANGE.

Many of our earthly problems come from the resistance to these three conditions. Our lives will be much easier if we can just learn to ACCEPT what is or what has happened and LET GO.

A book by neurologist Jill Bolte Taylor, M.D., that I have referenced before, called *My Stroke of Insight*, states that anger is only a "90 second phenomenon" in the brain. In other words, physiologically the brain only recognizes this condition for one and a half minutes. If you are angry longer than that, it is your choice. In this regard, Pema Chodron indicates that if you have uneasy or painful feelings or experiences, give them "90 seconds" and then be sure to "let them go." As Michael Singer referenced in his book, this ability to let these feelings and emotions go is opening the mind and heart. The goal of life is to open the heart as much as possible! The three instructions she gives to accomplish this are: (1) Become fully present, (2) Feel your heart (yes, put your hand over your heart), and (3) Engage in the next moment without an agenda.

As a Buddhist nun, Pema discusses at length "The Three Commitments" that all followers of her faith and practice believe and follow. Each of these commitments has a Tibetan name, which I will not use, but each stands for strong principles that most religions espouse, although not as deep and as stringent as her Buddhist practice.

THE COMMITMENT TO NOT CAUSE HARM.

As in most religions, these are commandments that tell you what NOT to do. The big three: NO craving, NO aggression, and NO indifference. The next list of NO's sounds something like the Judeo-Christian Ten Commandments. There is to be no killing! But in this tradition this does not just mean humans, it refers to animals (that's the reason for vegetarianism) and even bugs. All things that are have life and can move! To mirror the middle Commandments, there should be no stealing, lying, and no harmful sexual practices (not just adultery). Again, this practice goes one step further than the traditional Commandments in stating that there also should be no gossip, nothing to cause division or hatred, no cynicism, no sarcasm, and no condescension. And unlike the Judeo-Christian religions, there should be no alcohol or recreational drugs!

In the AA and Al-Anon program, the 4th Step is asking us to "make a searching and fearless moral inventory" of ourselves. This is backed up again in the 10th Step, when we are to "continue to take a personal inventory and when we were wrong, promptly admit it." In taking this First Commitment then, we would search out our behavior on a daily basis and if we realized we gossiped or were critical with another, we would make amends for our aberrant behavior as soon as possible. In the Buddhist tradition, this practice is called Sojong. Our overall goal with this First Commitment is to help heal others and benefit them in all possible ways. The basis of this practice is the process of MEDITATION, which centers us even if we can only do it for five to ten minutes a day. The 11th Step of AA and Al-Anon asks us to "seek through PRAYER and MEDITATION to improve our conscious contact with God."

As we live under this First Commitment, we are faced every day with "THE EIGHT WORDLY CONCERNS" or four sets of opposing conditions. They are PAIN versus PLEASURE, GAIN versus LOSS, FAME opposing DISGRACE and PRAISE versus BLAME. We are not to avoid any of these eight states but try to reside in the middle, or balance our condition at any point in time so we do not get off-center in our actions and reactions with others. As we desire not to cause harm to anyone (including ourselves!), we must not overreact or overact in any of our actions and reactions.

THE COMMITMENT TO SUPPORT AND BENEFIT OTHERS. This second commitment goes beyond the commitment to do no harm. Now we are talking about COMPASSION or the need to find ways to help others and get out of ourselves. It is the practice of looking of ways to serve others and think less of ourselves. The author makes reference to being a "shepherd" and making sure that all of the sheep are being cared for. In the New Testament, Jesus talks about the shepherd "leaving the ninety-nine sheep to go looking for the one lost sheep." Pema does not use this Bible reference, but it is exactly the same principle.

There was a book I read several years ago called *A Man Called Ove* by Scandinavian author Fredrik Backman. Last year it was made into a movie starring Tom Hanks, although the man's name was changed to Otto, probably for American audiences. The main character, portrayed by Hanks, was a miserable, irascible, cantankerous, and unkind man. He was the kind of person that some would hate and almost everyone else would avoid. However, his tiny Hispanic neighbor woman kept doing things for him, treating him kindly, and actually helping him to survive several suicide attempts. All this while keeping a cheerful and loving disposition in the process. This movie is the embodiment of the Second Commitment. The actress deserves an Academy Award for her role and behavior.

To relieve others of their emotional or physical pain, the Buddhists practice a ritual called "Tonglen." This is similar to meditation but is done almost as an "active" prayer to relieve the person or people that are going through the painful experience. The process starts with "breathing in" the pain of the afflicted person or people. And then "breathing out" flexibility, lightheartedness, non-aggression, and strength to the recipient. In the Al-Anon program, we listen to people living in an alcoholic situation and instead of giving them advice, we give them our "experience, strength (courage) and hope." This is the ultimate in getting out of yourself and serving those in need.

THE COMMITMENT TO EMBRACE THE WORLD JUST AS IT IS.
This is actually what the Al-Anon program is all about. The Serenity Prayer encourages us to "ACCEPT the things we cannot change," which means all sentient beings, places, and things. The only thing we can really change is ourselves. The First Step of AA and Al-Anon teaches us that "we are powerless" over alcohol, the alcoholic, and all others and that our lives have become "unmanageable" in trying to CONTROL, manipulate, and change things not in our purview. The key words here in my estimation are HUMILITY and SURRENDER. We must realize our limited capacity to avoid painful circumstances and maintain uplifting ones. The slogan "This too shall pass" is appropriate because all negative circumstances do pass, as do positive ones. We are directed to surrender to life, to turn toward whatever is happening rather than away from it. Embrace the "NOW" whatever it is and approach life with less FEAR and more acceptance and letting go.

One of my best friends as a dentist and a member of Al-Anon used to quote the song "Row, Row, Row Your Boat" when he gave a "lead" or shared his story of recovery in the program. You row your boat—gently, down the stream. You do not go against the current or fight the current! According to Pena Chodron, you stay in the "flow." You get away from the shore and stay in the middle of the stream and away from the two shores. You stay in the flow of life with no attachments, no avoidances, just living in the present and allowing.

As I mentioned earlier, this is the crux of the Al-Anon program. However, as a firm believer in the Al-Anon program, it would seem to me that if you are surrendering you need to have confidence in a Power that will take over when things are out of your hands. The Al-Anon slogan "LET GO, LET GOD" promotes the fact that without a Higher Power you have nothing to let go to. The Third Step of AA and Al-Anon states that "We made a decision to turn our will and our lives over to the care of God as we understand Him." In this Step we develop a TRUST in God that will allow us to let go and accept life's consequences without fear or anxiety.

The goal in living a life free of worry, fear, or angst is developing EQUA-NIMITY. This means you handle everything with CALM acceptance. In my forty-eight-year quest of "spiritual enlightenment," I have yet to achieve that state. Last week, I returned home from a meeting in Chicago and cut myself on my way to the subway. I had no bandage and was bleeding and I swore silently and obsessed over this wound. Then the subway came, we got on and traveled a few stops and then were ordered to get out of the train. I immediately panicked because I wasn't told why, and I was afraid I would miss my plane back to Cleveland. I was a hot mess for the next few hours even though I had plenty of time before my plane was to leave. If I truly followed the Three Commitments, especially the Third one, I would have been calm, accepting and a much happier (and healthier) person.

REALITY
LOVING WHAT IS
BYRON KATIE

"The only time we suffer is when we believe a THOUGHT that argues with WHAT IS" (capitalization mine).

"If I had one prayer, it would be this: 'God spare me from the desire for LOVE, APPROVAL, and APPRECIATION!'" (Again, caps mine).

Some of the authors that I am covering were actually "referred" to me by one of the other authors I have covered. Wise people appreciate wisdom from other wise people, and one of the authors I covered in this book (Brene Brown?) wrote that Byron Katie had a "process" of loving and living that was not to be missed. The book that describes this process is called *Loving What Is*, and I was informed that the concept would be lifechanging if I read the book and practiced the principles.

After making a mental note of this (I am sure I didn't write it down), I was visiting my son and daughter-in-law in Columbus for the evening. After dinner, they suggested we go to a "famous" local bookstore in the German Village section of town. Of course, I gravitated to the "inspirational," self-improvement section, which was a small room on the second floor in the multi-roomed two-story house that had become a bookstore. The first book I saw in the middle of the shelf that was exactly my height was *Loving What Is*. How I remembered the name of the book and author is one mystery, but how that book was presented to me at that time in that place in a bookstore I had never been in was somewhat of a miracle—maybe not just dumb luck or happenstance.

When you are in a recovery program such as AA or Al-Anon, your goal is to "work" the 12 Steps and of course the last or Twelfth Step outlines the final result. After developing a relationship with a Higher Power or God and then learning to "increase our conscious contact with that Power through prayer and meditation," as the Eleventh Step professes, we take the final step, which is "Having had a SPIRITUAL AWAKENING as a result of these steps, we carry this message to others and practice these principles in all our affairs." I truly believe the bookstore trip and the finding of *Loving What Is* was one of my now noticeable spiritual experiences.

My spiritual journey started in 1975, when my wife told me I "had" to go to Al-Anon if I wanted our marriage to last. Byron Katie's spiritual journey began in 1986, when she was hospitalized with an eating disorder and anger issues. At one time, she had to live in the attic of her house because of her caustic behavior and oppositional attitude. She had her spiritual experience that changed her life and that of many others, but there was no "program" or sage or Higher Power or God or notable condition that changed her thinking and acting.

Her concept is called "The Work" and it is a process of INQUIRY or asking questions to discover the truth of an idea or thought. Her revelation was that the ATTACHMENT to thoughts is what causes people to suffer, not the thought itself. The Work is a way of developing "non-resistance" to live life as it is or, in the words of the Al-Anon program, "life on life's terms." Although her belief in God or a Higher Power is in doubt after reading her book, she clearly points out that there are three types of events, thoughts, or "business." There is: (1) My Business, (2) Your Business, and (3) God's Business. Everything falls in those three categories and the only one we can change is (1) My Business. We have to totally accept the lack of control all of us have over other people's business or God's business.

The "Work" involves asking four questions about a thought and then asking the same question in three different ways, called "the turnaround." The questions to ask yourself are:

Is it true? Many things we take for granted or believe are not true, especially when it regards the thoughts and motivations of other people.

Can you absolutely know it's true? This question is necessary because most people think things are true until they are really pressed to commit that they have certainty about the absolute veracity of a thought.

How do you react, what happens when you believe that thought? Since most of suffering is caused by negative thoughts, the person usually feels some negative emotion and the exact emotion is emphasized to the questioner to show them how suffering is caused by a thought, even when it's not true.

Who would you be without that thought? This fourth question demonstrates to the person how great they would feel and how free they would be without the thought.

Then you try the three turnaround, which gives you further insight on other ways of relating to and thinking of the thought.

Byron Katie has many tools to help people do "The Work." She has a worksheet online, which allows the participant to write down "issues" they are having in life prior to using the four questions and turnarounds to work through them. These worksheets and other information can be found on the website *thework.com* or on the app that has been created. If you cannot learn to do the work by yourself, Byron Katie has a nine-day retreat to teach the concept in more detail.

The author suggests that you use the worksheet and do the process on your neighbor, spouse, friend, boss—another person—before you use it on thoughts about yourself. I will give an example from my own life that will hopefully help you see how the process goes.

"I have written three books and have given all four of my children copies and none of them have read them. I know they aren't readers (except my oldest son and his wife), but it's from their only living (elderly) parent and I thought they would read it because it is from me. They haven't even mentioned reading the introduction to the book. I feel slighted and minimized by their lack of effort and attention."

Byron would break down the "complaint" into several sections.

None of my children have read any of my books!

Is it true? Yes.

Can you be sure? No. They may have read one or a part of one, I really don't know.

How do I feel about that idea if it's true? Slighted, jilted, inconsequential.

How would you feel without that thought? Accepting, relieved.

Turnaround: All of my children have read my books.

I haven't read my books.

They "should" read my books because I am their only parent and I'm not getting any younger.

Is it true? No.

(Skip second question if first one is acknowledged as true.)

How do I feel if I believe they should read my books? Demanding, pressuring.

How would I feel without that thought? Accepting, freeing.

Turnaround: I should read my books because I'm the parent.

I shouldn't question their not reading the books.

This may not be a great example, but the Al-Anon program has taught me to accept and surrender to what is and how others feel. When my wife went back to using drugs and alcohol, I accepted it and was not angry. I was sad, but it was "her business" (and "God's business") and not "my business." The truth is, I was not terribly upset about my four children not reading my books, but I was a little surprised. Actually, my two "readers" may have read some of them and just not mentioned anything about them, which is perfectly fine. The truth is that they may decide to read one of them as a remembrance when the author is no longer around.

The bottom line is that there can be no SHOULDS or SHOULDN'TS or you MUST, or you NEED to. Katie tells the story about her son leaving his socks on the bedroom floor. She told him, "You must pick up your socks." Of course, the answer to the first question was NO, he did not have to pick up his socks. How do you know that's true? Because he didn't! Who wanted the socks picked up—Byron Katie! So she picked them up herself and it removed all that angst and stress. And eventually, her son started to pick them up without being ordered to.

Basically, if we think someone else is causing us pain, we're insane. We are the only ones who cause us pain with our faulty thinking and desire to CONTROL. The world is always as it should be and when we have a thought we need to ask ourselves if that thought gives us peace or does it give us stress and anger. Before Al-Anon, my wife was drinking and doing things that people with the disease of alcoholism do and I was racing around, trying to keep her from hurting herself and others. I was overstressed and over-worried about her activities as well as non-activities. One day I was trying to goad her into a different behavior pattern, and she wearily shouted, "What do you want from me!??" I tried to calm down and simply stated, "I want peace! I want peace of mind and freedom from worry and stress!" It took a few years in the Al-Anon program to realize that I was the only one who could give me peace. It was not hers to give me—she could only give it to herself. I am responsible for my peace, my happiness, my thoughts, and my actions.

Loving What Is discusses the value of forgiveness and making amends. Her son, who had done "the Work" for many years, admitted that as a youth he stole shirts from a particular store. To make amends, he purchased shirts from the same store and then put the shirt back on the rack in the store without the knowledge of the salesman. The Work is a humble program. It teaches us to listen without judgment. It proves the idea that "Everything happens For me, not To me!"

When you think people should be kind to you, use the turnaround and realize that you should be kind to them and yourself. Enemies are important because they help train us how not to behave and how to act in the face of opposition. They may be your greatest teachers in life. Even firing an employee may be the kindest thing to do for their benefit because it frees them to find a job that fits them and a place where they can thrive and advance.

Many of the sages we have read previously agree with the concepts of *Loving What Is*. The Al-Anon program fits this philosophy perfectly in that you can't CONTROL or CHANGE other people. In Al-Anon, we have the "hula-hoop" concept. If you hold a hula-hoop around your waist or drop it to the floor and stand in it, you can only change that which is inside the two-foot radius of the hoop. Again, the slogan that fits here is "ACCEPT, SURRENDER, LET GO." To go a bit beyond that concept in this book, I would add "ACCEPT, SURRENDER, LET GO, LET GOD." My thought is that unlike Our Business, God's Business is taking care of My Business and Your Business.

HEALING

OPENING OUR HEARTS, TRANSFORMING OUR LOSSES AL-ANON FAMILY GROUPS CONFERENCE-APPROVED LITERATURE

"An Al-Anon meeting may be the only safe place we have where we can speak from our hearts."

"I can't put closure on my feelings. Closure is something that happens to a home, not to feelings."

When my wife went to her first treatment program for the disease of alcoholism, she was told by her counselors that I should (had to) go to Al-Anon. If I had read *Loving What Is* by Byron Katie before my wife told me that I had to attend a program because I was affected by the family disease, I would have asked myself, "Is that true?" My answer would have been NO back then, and I might have missed out on a life-changing forty-seven-year spiritual journey.

Of course, since the suggestion or demand came from her treatment program, I erroneously thought that my attending weekly meetings of this program would make her recovery work or at least be smoother. God works in mysterious ways, and I was led to a meeting that gave me the principles to "love what is" and save my marriage and give me almost fifty years of serenity, peace, and hope—none of which I had at that time in my life. And it had nothing to do with my wife or her recovery.

The three things a Newcomer to the Al-Anon program learns at the first few Beginners meetings are: (1) The Three "C's," (2) Step One (of the Twelve Steps of AA and Al-Anon), and (3) the DISEASE of alcoholism and drug addiction. The three C's are: (1) I didn't CAUSE it, (2) I can't CURE it, and (3) and I can't CONTROL it! Since it is truly a brain disease, not a character weakness, the first two C's are easy to grasp. However, the Al-Anon member has trouble with the third C or Control. That is our "disease." We become so obsessed with the actions of the alcoholic that we do everything in our power to make them function "normally," as if they had no disease. Until we understand how the disease works, we will continue to attempt to control the addicts behavior and actions.

Step One of the AA and Al-Anon program tells us to "Admit we are POWERLESS over alcohol (and the alcoholic) and our lives had become unmanageable (because we struggled to control them)." Besides truly admitting our powerlessness, we use the SERENITY PRAYER to help us realize what our place is in relation to other people. "God grant me the Serenity to AC-CEPT what I cannot change, the COURAGE to change the things I can, and the WISDOM to know the difference." We are asking God to help us stop trying to control or change others and the courage to change just ourselves.

The Al-Anon program has many books that we use at the meetings and work from at home. We have three daily readers and a myriad of books and pamphlets, which help the members learn to "focus on themselves" rather than the alcoholic or any other person. We have bound workbooks that help us progress through the Twelve Steps so we can have the "spiritual awakening" that we are promised if we follow the principles of the program and attend meetings.

One of the many large softcover books we have is called *Opening Our Hearts, Transforming Our Losses*. People who are in a relationship with an alcoholic have many losses; some are minor and some major. In my case, I never really thought about all the losses I suffered and the grieving process until my ex-wife died at age seventy-one from her disease of alcoholism. This book really helped me "grieve" and gave me principles that made my landing so much softer. Of course, the people in the Al-Anon meeting rooms also gave me a place to discuss my feelings and reach out to in a vulnerable state. We call these Al-Anon members "God with Skin"!

We realize that even a large change in our lives can be a loss and require acceptance and even some grieving. When my wife recovered the first time and started attending AA meeting, I lost her to the new recovery program.

The men in AA were more important to her than I was and only the Al-Anon program kept our marriage together at that time. For me, and many others, especially men, the first year of recovery can be the hardest for someone living with a sober alcoholic.

Most of us have a "Dream" of life as we want it to be. We have EXPECTATIONS, which often do not work out, and we have to surrender to that form of loss. As a teenager, I was kept out of a club that all the cool guys were in and as a result, I isolated and felt the loss of belonging. The nice thing about Al-Anon is that belonging is easy because you are not voted on but welcomed and encouraged to participate. After reading the Al-Anon book on *Opening Our Hearts, Transforming Our Losses*, I started to realize there were other dreams I had, not only for myself but for my four children, which were not realized.

My two younger adopted children had to attend special boarding high schools out of state, so I incurred the loss of raising them during these crucial growing-up years. I also missed seeing them at proms and other events that occurred without my presence. Many of us in Al-Anon feel the loss of a close family relationship due to alcoholism in their family of origin so we turn to the Al-Anon "family" as our primary support family. Since the Al-Anon members have had the same experiences with alcoholics and addicts that we have had, they "open their hearts" to us to allow us to process loss and share our feelings of grief.

Money has never been a motivating factor for me. I have always been proud that I am not a spendthrift nor a tightwad. When I first started investing in the stock market, I thought I might fear losing money when the market dropped. The first time I lost a sizable amount of money, I was actually surprised that it did not bother me at all. For many people, the loss of money is the cause of grief, worry, fear, and angst.

I thought that I was not in that category until my wife, in an alcoholic fog, began using our savings to dole out money for houses and mortgages for friends and family members. When I addressed this over-generosity with her and said we needed that money to be sure our retirement was secure, she turned it into a negative, lose-lose confrontation, and nothing was solved.

The Al-Anon program deals a lot with fear and resentment, and I was in that latter category. I felt that to rid myself of the resentment over these exorbitant expenditures, I needed to "detach" or remove myself from the situation. I was able to accept my wife's struggle with the disease of alcoholism but not her doling out our retirement income, so I decided to move out of the house. Divorce or separation was not on my mind and if my wife "recovered" from the disease of alcoholism and financial irresponsibility, I would move back. Instead, she filed for divorce!

Again, because of the serenity I had achieved in the Al-Anon program, our divorce was an amicable one with no anger or retribution. When she wanted a bit more money to end the divorce, I gladly gave it to her. Three months after the divorce, she died of acute alcoholism. This double loss was very sad, but I was able to overcome it due to my Al-Anon sponsor and many friends in the Al-Anon program. I also had a counselor that helped as well.

Opening Our Hearts, Transforming Our Losses discusses in detail things we can do to overcome loss and grief. Journaling is one thing that is suggested but I have never been good at that, even though I am a writer. Other practices include prayer, meditation, the Steps, talking to your sponsor and having the courage to ask for help. We are to give the sponsor or other Al-Anon member the opportunity to help us and benefit from feeling good about helping a friend or program member.

Other practical suggestions from the book are: (1) proper exercise, eating habits and sleeping habits, (2) participation in hobbies or fun activities, (3) honoring your feelings, (4) allowing proper time to grieve, (5) increasing the number of Al-Anon meetings to attend, and (5) making more consistent use of Al-Anon literature like the one we are reviewing.

In regards to the time period for grieving a loss, Al-Anon suggests that there is no time limit and we all go through the process differently. But there was an experience in one of my meetings where a woman was grieving the death of her husband (not an alcoholic) for over a year. Her close Al-Anon friends saw that this extensive grieving was interfering with her life in many other ways, so they staged an "intervention." About six or seven Al-Anon ladies met with her and let her know that her process was now in overdrive, and it was overshadowing the rest of her life and activities. Friends in the Al-Anon program will do that for you, if necessary.

The Twelve Steps of AA and Al-Anon help us to recover from loss and turn our lives around for the better. Step Four asks us to make a "searching and fearless moral inventory of ourselves," and here we become humble and vulnerable in our quest to change our lives for the better. In Step Five, we discuss this introspective step with "God, ourselves, and another human being"—again asking for help and direction.

Sometimes in our loss and grief, our anger or discontent causes us to be unkind and hurtful to others. Step Eight asks us to "make a list of those we have injured and harmed" and then in Step Nine, we "make direct amends to those we have harmed." We also practice forgiveness. We ask for it when we make amends and if we are resentful or have hurt another, we give it.

The Al-Anon slogans that help a person who is dealing with grief and loss are: (1) "Easy Does It"—stay centered, stay calm, stay with God. (2) "One Day at a Time"—all we have to get through is the next twelve hours, keep your focus on the present. (3) "Let Go and Let God"—the program does not work without a Higher Power or God to rely on. (4) "How important is it?"—grieving people often get upset over very small and trivial issues, and the program reminds us about this with slogans such as these.

The program reminds us that no matter what we are grieving, we still have a lot to be grateful for. We need to focus on these things and thank God for the people and activities that are still in our lives. Besides gratitude for what we have, we are to have hope for the future. Hope is something I never had until I came to Al-Anon. Our little daily reader called "Hope for Today" has a quote that states: "In Al-Anon I've learned that despite all my losses, there is still hope."

Our first Al-Anon daily reader, "One Day at a Time," has a story (May 3rd) about a woman living in England at the time of the Blitz (1940) during World War II. Her husband had met sudden death in the bombing, and her minister went to break the news to her. When she greeted him she asked, "Are you bringing me bad news that you come at this unusual time of day?" "I'm afraid so," the minister answered. "Is it about my husband? Is he dead?" "Yes, I am sorry to bring you such sad tidings." She interrupted him to say, "Come in and let me make you a cup of tea." At his astonished look, she explained, "My mother taught me when I was a little girl that when anything very dreadful happens, I must think of *what I would be doing if it had not happened and then do that.*" Loss happens and grief follows, but we must move on and do the next best thing.

PERSPECTIVE
HORTON HATCHES THE EGG
DR. SEUSS

"Did he run? He did not! Horton stayed on that nest! He held his head high, and he threw out his chest. And he looked at the hunters as much as to say: 'Shoot if you must, I won't run away.'"

"I meant what I said, and I said what I meant. An elephant's faithful one hundred per cent!"

During my long orthodontic career, I attended a few courses in the latter years about retiring from the specialty. The usual advice was "Retire TO something, not FROM something!" In other words, those who retire and have nothing to do will languish and decline in health and longevity. I not only believed in this concept but felt that I had to come up with activities in retirement that really served others in healthy ways. For forty-six years, I had been creating futures for patients by giving them a smile that could promote them in relationships and the workforce.

My first outreach was to orthodontic departments close to me with the idea of teaching the young resident dentists who were specializing in the field of "dentofacial orthopedics." I secured parttime jobs in two departments: Seton Hill in Greensburg, Pennsylvania, and THE Ohio State University in Columbus. I had graduated twice from the school in Columbus and a young friend who graduated from the Seton Hill program helped me gain employment there.

But I also felt I needed a volunteer position where I could give my time and talent to a cause for no salary. I love children as has been mentioned, so it was natural for me to volunteer at Akron Children's Hospital as a "Roving

Reader." What that means is that I spend three hours a week reading to children who are patients in the hospital. And when I finish reading them a story, I give them a book to take home with them when they leave.

As a fan of books by Dr. Seuss, most of the books I read on Wednesday morning at Akron Children's come from that incredibly inventive children's author. The reasons I love these books are threefold: (1) They are nonsensical, (2) They all rhyme, and (3) They all convey a values-driven message of learning to the young listener. My favorites are *Yertle the Turtle*—turtles and all creatures should be free; *The Sneetches*—no matter which Sneetch has the star on his belly, they are equal in every regard; and *Horton Hears a Who*—a person's a person no matter how small.

But my favorite all-time book is *Horton Hatches the Egg*. It is one of three or four books the Doctor wrote about the elephant Horton, but it is the best example of FIFTEEN strong character traits or values that Horton displays in this wonderful story.

So when I read each book, whether from Dr. Seuss or *Clifford the Big Red Dog*, or *Curious George*, or *The Berenstein Bears*, I spend some time with the young patient going over the "message" of character development. And then I give them the book.

It would be hard to believe that any reader of this book would not know the story of how Horton hatched an egg, but I will run through it quickly and then go back and explain the message that is portrayed in the way Horton handles each situation.

It seems a lazy bird, Mayzie, is tired of sitting on her egg and would like an egg-sitter while she flies off to Florida for some R and R. Horton passes by and agrees to sit on the egg for her and does so without breaking it. He does not realize that Mayzie is not returning so he sits through storms, winter, and bullying by his friends because he "thinks he's a bird," according to the other animals in the jungle.

Then some hunters come along and decide that rather than shooting him, they will take him out of the jungle to New York and sell him to a circus for money because "he's terribly funny." In New York, he's sold to a circus and travels all over the U.S. as a side show for "10 cents a peek." That seems a bit low for a ticket to see an elephant in a tree, but the story was not written in modern times. The circus winds up in Florida and that lazy bird Mayzie sees the tents and decides she will go to the show. She swoops inside the tent and is shocked to see Horton on her tree and on her egg.

Just as she begins to challenge Horton for the rights to the egg she laid, the egg breaks open and reveals an "elephant-bird" who naturally flies over to Horton instead of Mayzie because Horton sat on the egg "faithfully for fifty-one weeks." They return Horton to the jungle with his new flying elephant infant and "it should be, it should be, it SHOULD be like that! Because Horton was FAITHFUL! He sat and he sat! He meant what he said, and he said what he meant. And they sent him home HAPPY, One hundred percent."

So what are the lessons that the story conveys to the young children I read to at Akron Childrens? GENEROSITY: Horton graciously gives up his time and efforts to help out the frustrated bird by volunteering to sit on her egg. He also proves to be HELPFUL and KIND. The second lesson or lessons would be COMMITMENT and DEPENDABILITY: The entire story is about his word being his bond—he does what he said he would do, no matter the time or the weather.

After sitting on the egg all winter, the spring comes and Horton's supposed friends come out of hibernation to play. They see him and begin to taunt and laugh at the "elephant up in a tree." There is a huge effort today to combat "BULLYING" and even though he is being bullied, he does not fire back and may even show a bit of TOLERANCE and FORGIVENESS.

Later in the summer, three hunters point their guns "straight at his heart." But does he run? He does not! "Shoot if you must, but I won't run away." Talk about COURAGE. The elephant has the courage to keep his word and do the right thing. When the hunters decide to put him in a cart and ship him to New York, he is not happy but shows ACCEPTANCE to what is and continues to be FAITHFUL to his word and "his" egg.

Besides showing the young readers the negative effects of bullying, the second negative trait is shown when Horton is sold "to a circus for money." GREED in this case was making money off a jungle animal even if he had to be relocated to a large city and carted around from city to city as a sideshow. No wonder they don't allow elephants to perform at circuses anymore! A value that Horton displayed that I cherish, although not good at, is EQUANIMITY. He was calm and accepting and even though he was carted around to almost every American city, he never complained or even "awfulized," as I tend to do.

When Mayzie flies down into the tent and sees Horton and realizes who he is and what he is doing, she screams at Horton: "It's my egg!" she sputtered. "You stole it from me!" (The work was all done. Now she wanted it back!) Then Horton showed unbelievable HUMILITY. He didn't argue or yell at Mayzie but "backed down with a sad, heavy heart." Of course at that very moment, the Universe (or God, as I would have it) took over and the egg hatched, producing a baby elephant that looked exactly like a little Horton, except it had wings.

At this point in my reading, I always ask the little child if they know of any other elephant that flies. About half of them brighten up and yell "Dumbo!" the Disney elephant. I then ask what the difference is in how they fly. Again, about 75 percent who answered "Dumbo" answered that Horton's baby uses wings and Dumbo uses his oversized ears.

As Horton returns to the jungle (we don't know how he gets back there from New York) with his new little "elephant-bird," we learn about PERSE-VERANCE. He sat on the egg for "fifty-one" weeks! This is when I ask the child how long a year is. I'm not sure why Dr. Seuss made Horton's effort one week short of a year, but it helps me in my teaching efforts. Because Horton was faithful, dependable, and committed, he receives the REWARD of par-enthood and the cheering (finally) of his fickle friends back in the jungle. The JOY he exhibits from doing the right thing and practicing all the righteous principles is one of the things that make Dr. Seuss' books so great and a valu-able teaching tool for children of all ages.

VALUABLE
DEVELOPING VALUES, DEALING WITH ISSUES
DR. MICHAEL J. BERNARD

"For me, a VALUE is a personal characteristic that allows one to be the best person he or she could be."

"My first lesson was that they did not have to read the entire Bible. All the lessons for a principled and worthy life are listed in just two of the sixty-six books—PROVERBS in the Old Testament and MATTHEW in the New Testament."

The Thirty Sages I have chronicled in this writing are the bulk of the wise men and women I have learned from and grown spiritually because of. This 31st "sage" is, of course, me! It may seem presumptuous of me to list myself as one who could teach the "Wisdom of the Sages," but then this is my book, so I have free license to end it with my own writing if I so please. After forty-seven years of learning from my mentors, the Al-Anon program and the sages I have reviewed in this book, I suppose I feel entitled to use one of my own books to demonstrate a sample of the wisdom I have gained.

When my wife went to treatment in 1975 for chemical dependency, she came home after four weeks and began attending Alcoholics Anonymous. Because of the codependency I had developed from living with an alcoholic father and an alcoholic wife, I was urged to attend weekly Al-Anon meetings to help me "recover." Both of these 12-Step programs are spiritual in nature, teaching that a relationship with a "Higher Power" or a God of our understanding could restore us to right thinking and acting and turn our lives around. At the age of thirty-five, I began to grow spiritually and in the process, I embraced religion as an aid to this growth direction.

After becoming confirmed in the Catholic Church, which my children were already involved in, I looked for some way to contribute to the faith and the church. I had never taught anything before but the staff or assistants in my orthodontic practice kept telling me I was a good teacher, so I thought I would investigate teaching religious education. As a neophyte Catholic, I really didn't know much about rituals and Sacraments, but I thought I could teach the kids morals, values, and decision-making that would help them in school and future endeavors. I become an orthodontist because I loved being with middle school-age children and helping them get ready for high school with more confidence due to a perfect smile and optimal facial balance. So I signed up to teach children in the thirteen-to-fourteen age range, which was the eighth grade or the year before they advanced to high school.

Thirty-five years later, I had a yearly curriculum for my students that included a list of VALUES that they should adhere to if they wanted to have good relationships and be successful in the business world. We also discussed some ISSUES that they would face in the future if they had not already faced them in middle school. I found twelve issues that they or their friends and family members would deal with in the future. The big lesson was that VALUES were consistent and non-changeable, but ISSUES had more than one right way to deal with them. I also had some other bits of wisdom that I would teach them, many lessons that came from some of the sages that are covered in this book. The three sources of my teachings were the Bible, the Al-Anon program and, of course, the wisdom of the sages.

The book I wrote is called *Developing Values, Dealing with Issues*, and it has three sections. Besides the Value section and the Issue section, there is a third section called "Extra Credit" because it comes from a middle school program. In my class and in this book, there are twenty-five Values that are discussed. There are also twelve Issues that these children will face, and there are eleven items in the Extra Credit section that come from "spiritual" lessons I have learned from books and people. In the review of this book, I will only touch on the five values I deem most important, the several issues I think are most pressing today, and two concepts in the Extra Credit section that are worthy of mention.

Starting with the most important five values out of the twenty-five discussed in the book, I will address each of the five in my order of importance.

The first and most important value is HUMILITY. If I had to sum up the Al-Anon program in one word, it would be "Humility." It has been said that humility is not thinking less of yourself, but thinking of yourself less. The sooner we realize that we do not have all of the answer to life's many questions and that we can rely on a Higher Power for answers and support, as well as human experts and people with more wisdom and experience than we have, our life will be much kinder and rewarding. Humility means that we are remaining teachable by others, and we can freely admit shortcomings and weaknesses that we must overcome. The Fourth Step in AA and Al-Anon is where we make a searching and fearless moral inventory and humbly admit that we have issues to be corrected and changed in our lives. And we cannot do this by ourselves. In the Fifth Step, we admit to God, ourselves, and one other human being the shortcomings or adverse character traits that we found in the Fourth Step. We must avoid Mohammed Ali's ringside rant that "I'm the greatest!" It's only when we admit we are not the greatest that our relationships and endeavors prosper.

Again, referring to the Al-Anon program and the Serenity Prayer, we only achieve serenity or peace of mind when we accept what is. Therefore, ACCEPTANCE is the second value that we must learn and practice. Not accepting what is or what has occurred leaves us angry and frustrated but doesn't change things. The ability to "accept what is" enables us to "respond rather than react." When we take the wrong exit on the freeway, lamenting about it does no good. We have to calmly figure out how to get back on the right route without awfulizing, swearing, or pounding on the steering wheel. I am much better at writing and understanding this than in practicing it! At my hospital volunteer job, I have to accept that over half of the children I attempt to read to will reject me. They have Mom's cell phone, tablet, and the TV, and an aging dentist with a low voice is not on their list of priorities. I call this Wednesday morning routine "rejection therapy." I must not take it personally but accept this turn-down gracefully and move on to the next room.

We do have a saying in the Al-Anon program that reads: "You don't have to accept the unacceptable." What this means is that you have to accept that someone treated you badly, but you can limit your exposure to that person as a way of avoiding something you would rather not accept again.

The Third most important value is TRUST. The Third Step of AA and Al-Anon tells us to "Make a decision to turn our life and our will over to God as we understand Him." This is the ultimate trust—that we come to believe that our Higher Power or God can be trusted with our will and our lives. Until we develop that trust in God, we find it hard to progress in the program and develop the serenity we so dearly seek. Developing trust takes time. Trust is earned, not just given like some of the other values. Once trust is betrayed, it takes a long time to earn it back. One of the reasons I left my home after forty-eight years of marriage was because when my wife relapsed back to using alcohol and pills, she began to use our money foolishly without my consent or knowledge. I really could not trust her with our savings, and I thought that also meant that I couldn't trust her with other things as well. Currently in our country, we are having a large trust issue with medical professionals, politicians, and religious organizations. We must gain wisdom from the right sources so our trust is not misplaced.

The fourth value would be RESPECT. I used to tell my Sunday students that, unlike trust, respect has to be given, not just earned. To demonstrate this, I would have a student come up to the front of the class and sit in a chair, which I told him or her was their car. I was the patrolman who pulled them over for speeding, and when they rolled down the "window" to address me respect had to be demonstrated. If they showed me respect, maybe just a warning; no respect, a ticket for sure. And if they were oppositional, maybe a trip to the police station. Our classroom was in the Catholic school and my students were all in public school except for Sunday mornings. They were told to respect the desk of the students whose desk they were using. They were to leave everything in good order and not go through any of the owner's books or school supplies. One of the main objectives of my class year was to teach them how much higher they would rise and how much more they would be accepted if they showed respect to all people, places, and things.

The fifth of the twenty-five in the book would be PERSEVERENCE. If one has a worthy objective, they should pursue it as long as possible. All of us have heard the story of the 1000 attempts Thomas Edison took to come up with the first lightbulb. Some years back, I read about a swimmer who attempted to swim the English Channel, which was thirty-five miles across. When he was twenty-two miles off the English coast, he gave up and swam back. He actually swam nine miles farther than his goal but never accomplished what he set out to do. When my wife and I decided to adopt two children, I was close to fifty years old. We were told we could not adopt from a local agency because of our age and almost all countries had forty-year-age-difference limits. This meant that at fifty I could adopt a ten-year-old, but my wife wanted a newborn. So we had to find our own child. An adoption attorney finally found us a woman who wanted to give up her child but when she was eight months pregnant, she changed her mind. At my wife's request, I called the obstetricians in our town and after three attempts and many months, we were able to adopt a newborn girl. For our second adoption, we found an agency that found babies in El Salvador, where any-age parent would suffice. After being matched with two that fell through, we finally hit pay dirt on the third. Not giving up was difficult but, in the end, very rewarding. My adopted daughter is now thirty-four and provided me with my only grandchild, and my Latin-American son is thirty-two and is getting married next year.

In the section of the book on ISSUES, the two biggest issues facing our country today are FEAR and DRUGS. Millions of people died during the COVID-19 pandemic due to the fear of being vaccinated. Some religions teach their members to fear sinning because they will go to a dark and hot place forever when they die. Politicians make laws out of fear of losing their power and their jobs rather than what is good for their constituents. There are more guns than people in the United States because people fear intruders and people different than them. And of course, the increase in firearms causes parents of young children to fear sending their kids to school—or even the supermarket. The increase of drug usage may even have some basis around fear. We are experiencing more overdose deaths from synthetic drugs than ever before. Medical professionals are prescribing more narcotics than necessary and the so-called "War on Drugs" was ineffective. I always warn my students about drugs including marijuana because if they are genetically predisposed to be an addict, just a little of a mood-altering drug could either ruin or take their life.

The third and last section of the book is called " Extra Credit," and the two items I think are most valuable are both diagrams. The first is called the "Y" DIAGRAM and symbolizes a large letter Y on the green board or Smartboard. The fork to the left on the Y is the "bad" or "wrong" side and the fork to the right is the "good" or right side. When the student comes to the fork in the Y or in life, they must decide which way to go. The diagram indicates that if they go to the left, it will bring them "Short-Term Gain" but "Long-Term Pain." If they choose the path to the right, they will be faced with immediate but Short-Term Pain and then a lasting period of "Long-Term Gain." Many examples were related to the students but since they are in middle school, the "cheating" issue was something they could relate to. If you cheat on a test and therefore pass without needing to study, you get an immediate short-term gain (you went left on the Y). However, when you are caught, you flunk, you lose credibility, you lose the knowledge you would have had if you had studied, and your character is tainted (maybe) forever. If you do not cheat (go up the right side of the Y), you may not get a very good grade (short-term pain) but you will learn that you have to study next time, your character and reputation will be intact, and your future is secure (long-term gain).

The "Give-Take Continuum" is another graphic that I used to teach the students what their goal should be in life as far as serving themselves and others. A long horizontal line is drawn on the board with a zero at one end and a 100 at the other end. This represents a person's lifespan. When you reside below the line in your journey through life, you are "taking" more than "giving." Above the line and you are giving more than you are taking. Obviously, at birth you can do nothing for yourself, so you are pretty far below the line. As you age, you begin to take care of yourself more each year until at some age, you cross over the line and now are giving to yourself and others more than you are taking. I would always ask my students, "At what age do people cross over the line from taking to giving?" Some would guess eighteen, some would guess twenty-one, but none of the fourteen-year-olds guessed their own age. "What if a fourteen-year-old had a father who left the family, a mother who was addicted and unable to function and a six-year-old that the fourteen-year-old had to take care of, feed, get ready for school, and help with lessons?" They were shocked to learn that a fourteen-year-old might have to be above the line. The object for them in life was to cross over the line at a reasonable age and then continue to rise as long as possible and not come down below the line again until age and disability required it.

The wisdom in this book was intended for young teen religious education students. Since there are many Biblical references in it, I'm not sure any public or non-Christian schools will be able to use it. I believe it would be useful in the homes of families who have weekly "family meetings" or family "spiritual sessions" like my family did. Pick a Value or Issue to discuss weekly at the meeting. If this ever happens, even on a limited basis, I will be able to consider myself the 31st Sage and maybe some people can learn from me.

EPILOGUE

In 1975, I was told by my wife that I needed to attend meetings of the Al-Anon program. This program is for "friends and relatives" of alcoholics. Of course, like many other "newcomers," I thought the program and meetings would tell me how to live with my now-recovering alcoholic wife and what I could do to keep her sober. I quickly learned that Al-Anon could help me focus on myself and my recovery from my worrisome, hands-on, controlling behavior. I had become obsessed with the alcoholic, even when sober, and my life needed as much help and correction as hers did.

The two things Al-Anon taught me that changed my life, and my perspective, were: (1) Alcoholism (and addiction) is a DISEASE. It is a chronic, non-curable, and fatal brain disease. The disease can be arrested but not "fixed." My wife was sober for thirty-five years and then the disease raised its ugly head again and she "relapsed"—from pills to vodka, which eventually took her life. The second thing I learned was that Al-Anon is a "SPIRIT-UAL" program, not a religious program. This has to be learned early because many newcomers either have no religious practice or they have had bad experiences with various religions they or their family participated in. In his first attempt at the program, my sponsor quickly got up and left when someone mentioned God!

So as I began to practice the Al-Anon program, using the meetings, readers, slogans, and Twelve Steps, I realized my quest was more SPIRITUAL than religious. The Steps prompt us to admit we are powerless over others, that there is a Power greater than ourselves who can help, and we need to decide to trust and turn our will and our lives over to that Power.

Al-Anon and the Steps call that Higher Power God, or the "God of my understanding." This means that as long as you have a belief in some "Spirit" that you can surrender to and admit that you need divine help, you can recover in the Al-Anon program.

Unlike many others in the Al-Anon and AA program, I found that religion helped develop my long-sought-after spirituality. I always felt closer to God when I was in a church whether alone or in a congregation. It is a quiet, almost sacred space where "believers" gather to pray together and meditate and grow in their relation to God. I have been in three different religions—two since my quest began in the Al-Anon program. All three of my religions are Bible based and Christian. However, there are thousands of religions and only one Al-Anon program. My Higher Power is Jesus Christ, but I resoundingly accept anyone else's concept of their Higher Power.

The 30 Sages I have reviewed in this writing are obviously not all religious and many who are are not Christian. Most religions have split off from other religions over the years because some of their members did not follow the exact precepts of that religion or had other ideas of how God worked and what the Bible really indicated. I believe that Judgment is in God's realm, not the religious hierarchy, and I believe that spiritual principles can be learned from many sources to gain wisdom and those who only use religious beliefs may be short-changing themselves spiritually. I have found in reading thirty books by spiritual authors that there are many religious and spiritual principles that are constant and longstanding and most of those just strengthen my Christian view. I only wish Christ could come back to earth for at least a day to sort out all the fear and animosity that politicians and some religions promote as "the way." Acceptance and kindness would seem to be the answers.

The benefit of covering thirty different spiritual authors is that you find recurring themes running through their philosophy that are shared with many of the other thirty sages. There were actually twenty-five principles that seemed to be emphasized by more than one of the sages. The most referenced was GOD, with a huge twenty-three authors talking about this divine Higher Power. Even the ones that were not total believers in God at least mentioned him as being relevant in wisdom and right thinking and action. There were three principles that had over ten authors espousing their use to gain personal mastery. The BIBLE had eleven, PRAYER had twelve, as did GOALS. Goals was the highest non-spiritual principle touted by the sages covered. The wisdom of the Bible is well known, and as a Christian I think the Sermon on the Mount (Matthew 5, 6, 7) is the greatest discourse on how to live a meaningful life and how to pray and relate to God and others. The other book in the Bible besides Matthew with Godly direction is Proverbs, which was written to dispense wisdom to the Hebrews in their new kingdom. The prayer that was used the most in many of the writings was the Serenity Prayer of the Al-Anon and AA program.

Coming in fourth was ACCEPTANCE with nine mentions. But two other similar principles—SURRENDER and NON-RESISTANCE—would have added another four to put Acceptance over nine authors as well. The other with nine mentions is THINKING. If you think you can, you can and if you think you can't, you can't. Negative thinking is discussed and discouraged. In the program, we call this "Stinking Thinking."

The next category would be those promoted by more than five of the thirty authors. There are five in that category, and they all are discussed by seven sages. The first is PRESENCE. We are taught to live in the present moment, not in the past or in the future. The present is all we have. The Al-Anon slogan for this is "One Day at a Time." The second is ACTION. Since the present is all we have, we need to decide what needs done right now, and act on it. As you recall, my slogan is "Just do it, and detach from the outcome." The Third principle with seven mentions is POSITIVE ATTITUDE. This is a choice we must make every moment of every day. This is helped by AFFIRMATIONS, which had three authors promoting them. The fourth with seven is SERVING. The goal (remember how important goals are) is to gain spirituality so we can serve God and other sentient beings. The last of the five with six authors is HUMILITY. I always tell people that if Al-Anon could be summed up in one word, it would be Humility. There is a God, and we are not Him.

Those principles with more than one mention were VISUALIZATION, COURAGE, ENTHUSIASM, MEDITATION, LISTENING, and FORGIVENESS. It is not surprising that these are the principles that I find most difficult in my life. I have never been good at visualization since I am an auditory person and my listening skills have never been one of my assets. My relationship with God and Jesus has allowed me to continue to develop the important spiritual principles of courage and forgiveness.

In reviewing what I wrote about each sage, there were three recurring topics that pervaded all the writings that I did not list as "principles." Two were negative themes that were often discussed as conditions to be avoided. As a recovering Al-Anon, the first one would be CONTROL. That is my disease. I seem to know what is best for my adult children, my one grandchild, my students, and my friends. That's where humility and God comes in. In the program, we use the "hula-hoop" image. If you place a hula-hoop around your waist and drop it to the floor, you are in control of only that which resides inside the hoop and nothing outside. The second negative concept is FEAR. In my humble opinion, this is the biggest problem facing mankind today! Gun violence is increasing daily because of fear of other people with guns. Parents are afraid to send kids to school and my daughter is even afraid to walk her son in the public park. We do not trust physicians, politicians, immigrants, or any government agency. Many of us are afraid of road rage and are afraid to smile at a stranger we pass on the sidewalk. This is where acceptance and Godly trust must enter.

The most important concept or theme that ran through all writing was that of LOVE. Love is a verb and the most important verb for mankind. Love alone will block out control and move us beyond this insidious increase in fear. We all can show more love to ourselves and, in this way, carry love to all those in the world outside. The most important part of my spiritual development was to discover that GOD IS LOVE, and the closer I am to him, the more likely I will be able to demonstrate this sacred concept.

The idea behind this writing is to allow the reader to read all the wisdom from all thirty sages or just pick one or two that they might relate to and see what they have to say. Many of the authors profiled here are not enticing or relevant to everyone's spiritual journey as they were to mine. As we say in the Al-Anon program, I am not giving you advice but only my particular philosophy and my experience in what I learned in my forty-eight-year spiritual quest. Again, a program slogan: "Take what you like, and leave the rest."

(SOME) OF THE BOOKS
OF THE SAGES
(REFERENCED VOLUME UNDERLINED)

Norman Vincent Peale: <u>The Power of Positive Thinking, Why Some Positive Thinkers Get Positive Results, You Can if You Think You Can, The Power of Positive Living, Enthusiasm Makes the Difference, The Amazing Results of Positive Thinking</u> (more than sixty books in all!)

Earl Nightingale: <u>The Strangest Secret, Lead the Field, The Essence of Success</u> (many taped programs through Nightingale-Conant)

Dennis Waitley: <u>The Psychology of Winning, Seeds of Greatness, The Winner's Edge, Empires of the Mind, Being the Best, Psychology of Success, The Joy of Working</u>

Zig Ziglar: <u>Over the Top, Secrets of Closing the Sale, See You at the Top, Goals!, Embrace the Struggle, Born to Win, Selling 101</u>

Jim Rohn: <u>My Philosophy for Successful Living, 7 Strategies for Wealth and Happiness, Twelve Pillars, The Seasons of Life, The Power of Ambition, Exceptional Living</u>

Matthew: The Sermon on the Mount, the rest of the first book of the New Testament

Wayne Dyer: Change Your Thoughts, Change your Life; Living the Wisdom of the Tao, Your Erroneous Zones, The Shift, The Power of Intention, Manifest Your Destiny, Wishes Fulfilled, You'll See It When You Believe It

Jack Canfield: The Key to Living the Law of Attraction, The Success Principles, Chicken Soup for the Soul (numerous *Chicken Soup* books)

John Maxwell: Three Things Successful People Do, Laws of Leadership, Five Levels of Leadership, Developing the Leader within You, Failing Forward

Don Miguel Ruiz: The Four Agreements, The Mastery of Love, The Voice of Knowledge, The Fifth Agreement, The Five Levels of Attachment

Deepak Chopra: How to Know God, The Seven Spiritual Laws of Success, Abundance, Perfect Health, Quantum Healing, Living in the Light, Creating Abundance

Eckhart Tolle: The Power of Now, A New Earth, Stillness Speaks, Practicing the Power of   Now, Becoming a Teacher of Presence, Oneness with All Life

Tony Robbins: Awaken the Giant Within, Unlimited Power, Life Force, Money – Master, The Game, Unshakeable, Unleash the Power Within, Giant Steps

Dan Millman: The Way of the Peaceful Warrior, The Life You Were Born to Live, The Journey of Socrates

Stephen Covey: The 7 Habits of Highly Effective People, The Leader in Me, The Eighth Habit, Principle Centered Leadership

Mitch Albom: The Five People You Meet in Heaven, Tuesdays with Morrie, The Stanger in the Lifeboat

Andy Andrews: <u>The Final Summit, The Traveler's Gift, The Noticer, The Seven Decisions, The Butterfly Effect, The Heart Mender, The Lost Choice</u>

Max Lucado: <u>Unshakeable Hope, You Are Special, Be Anxious for Nothing, Help Is Here, He Gets Us, You'll Get Through This, Traveling Light</u>

Gary Chapman: <u>The Five Love Languages, The Four Seasons of Marriage, The Five Languages of Apology, The Five Love Languages for Children</u>

Gary Smalley/John Trent: <u>The Blessing, The Language of Love, The Two Sides of Love, The Gift of the Blessing, Love Is a Decision</u>

Henry Cloud: <u>9 Things You Simply Must Do, Boundaries, Necessary Endings, Safe People, Changes That Heal, Boundaries in Marriage, Boundaries Workbook</u>

Joel Osteen: <u>Next Level Thinking, I Declare, The Power of I Am, Rule Your Day, Peaceful on Purpose, Empty Out the Negative, You Are Stronger</u>

Brene Brown: <u>The Gifts of Imperfection, Dare to Lead, Daring Greatly, Rising Strong, Braving the Wilderness, Atlas of the Heart, The Power of Vulnerability</u>

Simon Sinek: <u>Start with Why, The Infinite Game, Leaders Eat Last, Leaders, Know Your Why: How to Find Your Place in the World</u>

Mel Robbins: <u>The 5 Second Rule, The High Five Habit, Take Control of Your Life, Stop Saying You're Fine, Work It Out</u>

Michael Singer: <u>The Untethered Soul, The Journey beyond Yourself, The Surrender Experiment, The Search for Truth, Living Untethered</u>

Pema Chodron: <u>Living Beautifully, When Things Fall Apart, The Places That Scare You, Start Where You Are, How We Live Is How We Die</u>

Byron Katie: <u>Loving What Is, The Four Questions, Friendly Universe, A Thousand Names for Joy, Who Would You Be without Your Story?</u>

Al-Anon: <u>Healing Our Hearts, Transforming Our Lives, How Al-Anon Works, One Day at a Time, Courage to Change, Hope for Today, Discovering Choices</u>

Dr. Seuss: <u>Horton Hatches the Egg, Horton Hears a Who, The Lorax, The 500 Hats of Bartholomew Cubbins, The Cat in the Hat, Green Eggs and Ham</u>

Michael Bernard: <u>Developing Values, Dealing with Issues, Make It Better, Wooden Swing Sets</u> (unpublished)